Published on the Foundation Established in Memory of Oliver Baty Cunningham of the Class of 1917, Yale College.

By the Same Author

MAHAN

THE LIFE AND WORK OF
CAPTAIN ALFRED THAYER MAHAN

THE

ARMED FORCES

OF

THE PACIFIC

A COMPARISON OF

THE MILITARY AND NAVAL POWER

OF THE UNITED STATES

AND JAPAN

By Capt. W. D. Puleston, U.S.N.

NEW HAVEN
YALE UNIVERSITY PRESS
1941

TO

The Armed Forces of the United States

FOREWORD

THERE is a tendency in the United States at the time of writing to look upon the Pacific problem as of secondary importance. This is due in part to the desperate struggle in Europe, and the intention of this country to render all possible aid to Great Britain. It is also partly due to a lack of knowledge of the importance of our interests in the Pacific, and of the situation in that area.

Such an attitude is believed to be a serious mistake. The United States has vast interests in the Pacific. In 1937 one fourth of our foreign commerce was with the Far East. We depend entirely on that area for some of our most important raw materials. Our nationals have traded with China for more than one hundred and fifty years. We have cultural interests that have done much to promote understanding and friendly relations.

We have our flag flying in the Philippines and are in duty bound to defend them until they achieve their independence in 1946. The granting of this independence proves definitely that we have no imperialistic aims.

Our foreign policy is not one of imperialism, but one of mutual tolerance and fair dealing. We ask no special privileges, either in the Far East or any other part of the world. This policy is clearly defined by the Secretary of State as follows:

In our relations with the Far East as elsewhere this country has had two main ends in view: The promotion and protection of legitimate American rights and interests of other countries; and the furtherance of peaceful and mutually beneficial relations among the members of the Family of Nations. In seeking to attain these ends, this country has favored equality of opportunity, respect for national sovereignty, and faithful observance of treaties as the bases of a really durable international order.

The policy of Japan since the restoration differs greatly from that enunciated by Secretary Hull. It has been one of expansion by force of arms, mainly at the expense of China. Now, due to the situation in Europe, the Japanese militarists see the opportunity to realize their dreams of a vast, self-contained empire, embracing the entire Far East, from which all other nations will be excluded. It will be an empire, maintained by force of arms, whose millions of subjects are in the status of serfs.

In pursuance of this aim, a war has been carried on in China for nearly four years, resulting in the death of millions of innocent people and incredible suffering to many millions more. Japan herself has had nearly two million casualties in her army, and her people at home have been saddled with a debt that cannot be recovered from occupied territories for many years, if ever. The tragedy of this war in the East is that Japan could have achieved her aims of commercial dominance by peaceful means and by a policy of friendship toward China.

It is incredible that a great nation such as China, with traditions and culture reaching far back into the centuries, will ever willingly accept the rule of a foreign power. The extraordinary resistance of the Chinese to a far superior military force during the present war is sufficient proof that Japan can never achieve victory.

The problem of American and Japanese statesmen is to reconcile two apparently irreconcilable policies. Japan aims at exclusion and military control over areas in which we are vitally interested. The United States wishes only equal rights and opportunity for our citizens and our commerce. Yet we are firm in our intention to defend those rights. For the sake of the people of Japan and those of the United States it is profoundly to be hoped that a settlement satisfactory to both nations will be achieved.

This volume sets forth clearly and concisely the policies influencing the relations of the United States and Japan, and the armed forces at their command.

The author is thoroughly qualified to deal with this subject. As a naval officer he has served on the Asiatic Station as a part of his sea duty. He is a graduate of the Naval War College, and for several years was in charge of the Office of Naval Intelligence in the Navy Department. His biography of Admiral Mahan establishes his position as a distinguished authority on naval history and strategy.

H. E. YARNELL, *Admiral*
U.S.N. retired.

PREFACE

IN this book the probabilities of war and peace between the United States and Japan are considered and certain situations that might arise in the event of war are discussed. The author does not believe war between the two countries is either inevitable or unthinkable; he is convinced that a careful appraisal and a calm discussion of the factors that lead toward war and those that tend toward peace will assist in prolonging the friendly relations that have long existed between Japan and the United States.

A determined effort has been made to give a fair statement of Japan's policies and purposes in the Far East, and to submit an accurate estimate of Japan's military might. Actual figures of Japanese military and naval forces are carefully guarded state secrets, and those given in this text must be accepted with reservations. The comparison of the over-all strength of Japan with that of the United States is believed to be substantially correct; comparative values are essential for military decisions depend upon relative rather than absolute strengths.

Japanese-American relations have been marked by periods of extreme tension, succeeded by eras of goodwill, which in turn have been followed by other periods of strain. Between the Russo-Japanese War and the outbreak of the World War in 1914 there were several acute crises; only by the indefatigable efforts of intelligent statesmen on both sides was war averted on those occasions.

These statesmen have been assisted by the feeling of mutual respect existing between Japanese and American army and naval officers; if war comes, officers of both countries realize they will confront skilful, resourceful and courageous opponents who will prove formidable adversaries. Japanese and American armies and navies have proved their skill, courage and patriotism on many occasions, and their officers are under no obligation to reassert these qualities by dragging their countrymen into an unnecessary war.

The Japanese regard their exclusion from the United States as a national affront and deeply resent our attitude toward their race.

They feel that without adequate justification
the United States has repeatedly opposed their
necessary efforts to expand in Manchuria and
China. Americans on the other hand have
been outraged by Japan's treatment of the Chinese, and by the disregard of American life
and property shown by the Japanese troops in
China. Nevertheless the United States has accepted threadbare explanations from Tokio
for the series of attacks on Americans that culminated in the bombing of the U.S.S. *Panay*.
These two high-spirited peoples have shown
surprising patience with each other in times of
crisis; by their mutual forbearance the Japanese and American people themselves have
made the greatest contribution toward peace,
and in their national self-restraint lies the surest hope for future peace between the two nations in the difficult days ahead.

I wish to express my appreciation to Prof.
Harry R. Rudin, of Pierson College, Yale University, for his valuable aid and excellent suggestions in preparing the manuscript; to Eu-
gene A. Davidson, Editor of the Yale University Press, for his cordial coöperation and his
encouragement to undertake this work; to

Ella Holliday, Roberta Yerkes and Richard Tweedy for their editorial assistance, and to Alice Streator Fenton for her secretarial assistance. I should like to thank Colonel Claude H. Miller, U. S. Army, Retired, Commander Arthur H. McCollum, U. S. Navy, and First Lieutenant Andrew M. Kamarck, U. S. Army Reserves, for their advice and assistance.

W. D. P.

Mountain Lake Club
Lake Wales, Florida.
March 15, 1941.

CONTENTS

CHAPTER ONE

THE RISE OF JAPAN

AMERICANS occasionally overestimate the influence of Commodore Perry in removing the barriers between Japan and the outside world in 1853. The Dutch, the French, the Russians and the English also actively participated in reopening Japan to foreign trade. Internal forces, undoubtedly connected with increasing population, were germinating in Japan for a half century before Perry's visit and eventually would have compelled the Japanese to emerge from their voluntary seclusion. In the decade and a half preceding Perry's visit a severe domestic depression accelerated these expansive internal factors. Economic conditions resulted in great distress for the favored warrior class, many of whose members were reduced to poverty. The *ronin,* those dependent nobles who for some reason had become outcasts, often found that only by banditry was it possible for them to maintain a livelihood.

The question of reopening the country to foreign trade to relieve the domestic situation was widely agitated and the supporters of this policy organized a party under their own national leaders.

The readiness of numerous Japanese to participate in world affairs is not surprising, for the term of their seclusion, a little more than two centuries, is a small span of their national life. Traditionally the Japanese are good sailors and expert deep-sea fishermen; long before they voluntarily restricted their activities to their own shores, they had navigated the surrounding seas, explored the adjacent coasts, and vigorously participated in the affairs of their neighboring countries. Seclusion was not in accord with their inquisitive and acquisitive character, and the rapidity of their expansion since 1853 is evidence that their reëntry into the world was in accord with the natural genius of the Japanese people themselves.

In 1876 Japan reëstablished her jurisdiction over the Luchu Islands which had been contested by China. She had already reasserted her sovereignty over the Bonins, which had been occupied by descendants of whalers and their Hawaiian wives. These settlers had claimed the islands for Great Britain. Japan had less success in negotiations with Russia which, in return for the barren Kuril Islands and a small loan, forced her under the threat of war to abandon claims to any part of Sakhalin Island or the coasts of Siberia. Japanese statesmen learned from that experience that Russia's policy of expansion southward was Japan's greatest peril; since that time Japan has carefully scrutinized every Russian move in the Far East.

In opening Korea to foreign trade Japan demonstrated that she was an apt pupil of Europe and the United States. In 1876 she dispatched a naval expedition to Korea and compelled the Korean court to enter into a treaty, following closely the methods used by Commodore Perry. Among the terms were included extraterritorial clauses like those Perry had forced on Japan.[1]

Japan fought China for Korea and South Manchuria in 1894–95 and was deprived of Port Arthur and Manchuria by Russia, France and Germany. Russia continued to oppose her efforts to gain complete control of Korea. After the Japanese connived at the murder of the

1. Stanley K. Hornbeck, *Contemporary Politics in the Far East* (New York, D. Appleton & Co., 1916), pp. 199–200.

Korean Queen in 1895, the King took refuge in the Russian legation. A diplomatic struggle began between Russia and Japan for control of the country and for a time Russia supplanted Japanese influence there. In 1896 the Lobanov-Yamagata agreement established a condominium, but the rivalry between Japanese and Russians continued, both persevering in their intrigues to gain unchallenged authority. The persistence with which Japan followed her policy of expansion into Korea foreshadowed a similar doggedness of purpose which she has displayed in her invasion of Manchuria and China.

Japan was no servile copyist of occidental methods of expansion; she embellished them with some ideas of her own, and in Korea employed both oriental and occidental means to divide the Korean people into factions and to corrupt the court and ruling class. Korea was Japan's first major conquest; her pioneering system was successful and she used it as a model for her subsequent invasions of Manchuria and China.

Japanese expansion was not limited to the Far East. A diplomatic struggle between Japan and the United States for control of the Hawaiian Islands was in progress when Japan fought China in 1894. Japanese immigrants to those islands increased from 116 in 1883 to 24,000 in 1896, when they constituted almost one quarter of the population. Practically all these immigrants were adult males and formed a Japanese colony described by Rear Admiral John G. Walker as a solid body of brave men, with natural military instincts, who would fight if aroused and whose leaders were believed to have political ambitions.

In 1896 Rear Admiral Daniel Ammen wrote, "It does not require a prophet to foresee that those islands in the near future will be either American or Japanese." In 1897 Secretary of State John W. Foster referred to the rising power of Japan as a menace to the independence of the republic set up by Americans under President S. B. Dole.[2] In 1898 when the United States annexed the islands the Tokio Government forwarded a formal protest, which still reposes in the State Department, available if Japan ever wishes to reopen the discussions. The United States won this first skirmish and

2. See Edwin A. Falk, *Togo and the Rise of Japanese Sea Power* (New York, Longmans, Green & Co., 1936), pp. 135-136.

secured control of the eastern Pacific without serious opposition because the continued progress of Russia into Manchuria and her threatening advance toward Korea compelled Japan to concentrate on affairs in the western Pacific.[3]

"It was Japan's forward policy that brought on the Chino-Japanese War of 1894."[4] By her defeat of China in 1895 Japan acquired Formosa, the Pescadores, and South Manchuria, exposed the impotence of the imposing-looking Chinese Empire, and precipitated the attempted European dismemberment of China just before 1900. The Germans occupied Kiau Chau in November 1897. A month later the Russian Fleet steamed into Port Arthur and remained for the winter. In the ensuing spring China ceded Kwangchow Bay to France and offered no resistance when Great Britain oc-

3. Commodore Perry had refused the offer of the commander of a Russian squadron in China to coöperate in the opening of Japan, and except in 1918, when the United States assisted the White Russian armies, we have never actively collaborated with Russia. Yet Russo-American interests have frequently coincided in the Far East. The policies of Russia have had a large and continuous effect on Japanese-American relations, and today the attitude of Russia is one of the major factors in the struggle to protect American interests in the western Pacific.

4. Hornbeck, op. cit., p. 220.

cupied Weihaiwei, across the Yellow Sea from Port Arthur, whence the British Asiatic Fleet could observe the movements of the Russian Fleet based there.

When John Hay returned from the United States Embassy in London to become Secretary of State he was familiar with the current European rivalries for spheres of interest in China. Dewey's victory in Manila Bay and our subsequent occupation of the Philippines increased the already considerable American interest in the China trade. With a small outlay Manila could have been made a secure gateway for American commerce with the Far East. A desire to promote American trade and a genuine sympathy for helpless China inspired Hay's negotiations with the great powers from which was evolved the open-door policy. In March 1900 Hay formally notified Great Britain, France, Germany, Italy, Japan and Russia that, *in his opinion,* each of these six powers had entered into an agreement with the United States which amounted to a mutual pledge to preserve the commercial *status quo* and to refrain, each in what might be its sphere of interest, from measures calculated to destroy equality of opportunity.[5] Japan, preparing systematically for a war with Russia, did not protest the American occupation of the Philippines and increased American participation in Far Eastern matters, for the United States usually coöperated with Great Britain and Japan in their diplomatic opposition to Russian encroachments on Chinese territory.

Great Britain had already established a commercial base, which included a free port open to the trade of all nations, on the small island of Hong Kong. This form of occupation was quite different from the physical seizure and exclusive possession of Chinese provinces that characterized the expansion of Japan and Russia into China. It may be said that Russia began the dismemberment of China in 1858 and 1860, and about fifteen years later Japan renewed the policy of encroachment on China's territory. Nevertheless, her occupation of Hong Kong made it difficult for Britain to offer any moral objection to other nations' improving upon an example she had set. Japan, still in the process of absorbing Formosa and the Pescadores and strengthening her position

5. *Ibid.,* p. 235.

in Korea, was not strong enough to fight Russia or to oppose the European powers in China. Accordingly, Great Britain and Japan were glad to follow the lead of Hay and lent their diplomatic support to the open-door policy, although the Japanese Government was already committed to a policy of expansion in Asia and had itself continued the dismemberment of China. Russia, by establishing herself in South Manchuria after ejecting Japan, opened the struggle which is still in progress between them for Chinese territory.

Japan and the United States participated with the other great powers in the relief of Peking during the Boxer rebellion of 1900. During the next four years Russia continued her advance into Manchuria, encouraged by Germany. For this policy Germany had various understandable motives: namely, to win Russian friendship, to keep Russia (always a potential enemy as an ally of France) out of Western Europe, and to counterbalance England's strength in the Far East. For reasons of European diplomacy France was disturbed by a Far Eastern venture that reduced Russia's value as an ally. It was at this time that France turned to England and began in January 1902 those negotiations that eventually led to the Anglo-French entente.

The United States, after the Boxer rebellion, continued to take the lead in defending the territorial integrity of China. At this time Great Britain and Japan supported the position of the United States; Japan entered into a formal alliance with Great Britain in 1902, and continued her preparations to meet Russia. During the decade preceding the Russo-Japanese War Japanese-American relations were cordial and friendly, and throughout the war Americans sympathized with Japan. In fact, Japanese bonds sold in New York City helped to finance the war costs.

Between 1893 and 1905 Japan defeated two huge continental empires, China and Russia; she revealed to the world the universal corruption, the governmental inefficiency, the military and naval incompetence that existed under the absolute rule of the Manchu dynasty and the house of Romanov. Japan's victory over the Manchus had precipitated the European rush to dismember China; her victory over the Romanovs reduced the power of Russia and correspondingly increased the influ-

ence of Germany and the Triple Alliance in
Europe.

Russia's defeat in 1905 showed England that
Russia was no longer in a position to threaten
British interests in the Far East. To meet that
threat England already had the support of
Japan; their alliance of 1902 was renewed in
1905 and expanded to include India. Now that
the fear of Russia had been removed, England
desired to keep Russia from entering any com-
pact with Germany. England's entente with
France in 1904 made a *rapprochement* with
France's Russian partner a practical possibility
in 1907. Thus the Triple Entente came into
being, a system of bilateral arrangements between England, France, and Russia. In fact,
one may think of it as a quadruple entente, because by 1907 Japan had bilateral arrangements with each of these three powers. In this
way Europe came to recognize the growing importance of Japan in world politics.

After 1900 the wave of Japanese immigration swept from Hawaii to the west coast of
North America. The successful conclusion of
the war with Russia in 1905 coincided with renewed agitation on the Pacific coast of the
United States for excluding the ever-increas-

ing Japanese immigrants. Relieved of the Russian menace, Japan did not hesitate to express her resentment of the proposed treatment of her nationals; some of her papers advocated war with the United States. Several times during 1906 and 1907 the tension between the two nations was acute. The defenses at Manila were continuously on the alert. In the spring of 1907 the Armored Cruiser Squadron of the United States Asiatic Fleet operating off Chefoo under command of Rear Admiral James H. Dayton was followed for several days by a division of Japanese battleships and a flotilla of destroyers. Mindful of the surprise attack delivered by the Japanese against the Russians three years before, the American admiral kept his squadron cleared for action day and night.

President Theodore Roosevelt took personal charge of Japanese-American negotiations, and carefully explained to the Japanese Ambassador that economic reasons compelled the United States to exclude Asiatics; he made a great effort in the Gentlemen's Agreement to soothe the injured pride of a proud people and almost simultaneously he ordered the Atlantic Fleet of sixteen battleships to the Pacific. The cruise of the fleet was extended to include a visit to Japan, where its friendly reception and the sympathetic and determined efforts of the two governments temporarily relieved the tension.

The problem of immigration was quieted down for the time being, only to flare up in 1913 on account of laws passed in California applying to all aliens, but intended to restrict the activities of the Japanese. Their pride deeply hurt, the Japanese people were openly resentful and their press talked of war. In February 1915 the Foreign Minister of Japan, Baron Kato, stated with as pointed words as diplomacy permits that "the question . . . is a very irritating one" to the Japanese people, who "think ourselves ahead of any other Asiatic people and as good as some of the European nations."[6]

The war of 1914–18 removed all European restraint from Japan; except for our diplomatic pressure she had a free hand in China. After her capture of Tsingtao and the German islands in the North Pacific she concentrated her energies upon her own industrial development; war orders from Europe financed the establishment of her heavy industries; she in-

6. Quoted in Hornbeck, *op. cit.*, p. 379.

creased her merchant marine and occupied the foreign markets abandoned by European belligerents. Most of all she extended her influence into China. The war years were golden ones for Japan; the cost of her war effort was negligible, but as a nominal ally she was allowed to send military and naval observers abroad where they missed none of the lessons of the war. Stimulated by her easy conquests, she determined to exploit the opportunity and made the afterward celebrated Twenty-One Demands upon China in 1915. But for the United States, which forced the elimination of one group of these demands, China would have been absolutely helpless. As it was, she was forced to sign an agreement which even in its diluted form gave Japan a dominant control of her economic life.

Japan has labored in vain to get the United States to acknowledge her claims to predominance in the Far East; she thought she had succeeded after Viscount Ishii obtained the signature of Secretary of State Lansing to the Lansing-Ishii memorandum, which included the statement that "the government of the United States recognizes that Japan has special interests in China." The reluctant assent of Lansing was conditioned on Japan's promise to respect the open door and the independence and territorial integrity of China. Japan almost immediately used this note to increase her pressure on China, which informed the United States of the action. The history of the Lansing-Ishii memorandum is not creditable to either nation, and it was terminated in April 1923 by the provisions of the Washington Naval Treaty.

Japan's last big chance for expansion came during the World War but was blocked by the United States. Ostensibly an ally of England, France and Russia, Japan took continuous advantage of them all and but for the resolute action of President Wilson, who insisted that the territorial integrity of Russia be respected, would have exploited the confusion that followed Kerensky's downfall to seize parts of Siberia.

In the Washington agreements of 1921–22 the United States, backed by Canada and Australia, brought the Anglo-Japanese alliance to an end. It also sought to obstruct Japan's expansion in China by an international agreement to "respect" the sovereignty, independence, and territorial and administrative integrity of China. Japan, already troubled by Chinese passive resistance, felt compelled to restore Shantung to China. A limit was set to naval armaments, with Japan placed in an inferior position to England and the United States. These checks came primarily from the powers that had rejected Japan's demand for racial equality at Versailles.

Today the United States is the only stumbling block in the path of a still greater Japan. Again the United States finds itself almost against its will placed in a position where it must either actively oppose Japan or see within a few years the dream of Japanese imperialists fulfilled. Inaction on the part of the United States will be fraught with as momentous consequences as action. If the United States did nothing Japan could overrun Indo-China, Malaya and the Dutch East Indies. The Philippines would be isolated and Australia at the mercy of Japan.

Since the 'twenties Japan has set the pace for the dissatisfied nations; she defied the

League of Nations and marched into Manchuria in 1931, four years before Hitler denounced
the disarmament clauses of the Versailles
Treaty and five years before Mussolini invaded
Ethiopia; she announced her intention of
withdrawing from the League of Nations in
May 1935, four months before the Germans
withdrew; she broke the peace in China in
1937, two years before Hitler marched into
Poland. In these years Japan has been the pio-
neer, Germany and Italy her imitators, following her example in attempting to set up a new
order in Europe and Africa based on force and
modeled after Japan's new order in Asia and
the Far East.

In the past decade the development of the
heavy industries in Japan has been extraordinary; before 1929–30 her principal industrial
products were textiles, pottery, food process-
ing, consumers' goods, and paper; by 1935
metals, chemicals, machinery and engineering
products accounted for almost 50 per cent of
her production, about 55 per cent in 1937, and
about 61 per cent in 1938. Japan produces her
own ships, many of her airplanes, a large part

of her steel, arms, ammunition, and fertilizers; she still imports many automobiles and their parts, and a substantial percentage of the raw materials that feed her industries. Because of her lack of raw materials, since 1937 Japan has endeavored to develop the resources of Manchuria, China and adjacent regions in the Pacific.[7]

Foreign Minister Arita is quoted in a consular report as having in November 1938 disclaimed any intention of establishing an economic monopoly in Manchukuo, explaining that the purpose of closer economic relations between Japan, Manchukuo and China was to assure the supply to Japan of certain necessary products. But he finally stated that "it might become necessary to grant certain [Japanese] industries monopolistic privileges as a means of protection. In such cases, . . . foreigners will not be allowed to establish competitive businesses . . ." Japan proposed "to place herself in a position of security against the possible application of sanctions . . . by nations inside or outside of the League of Nations,"

7. E. B. Schumpeter, ed., *The Industrialization of Japan and Manchukuo, 1930–1940: Population, Raw Materials and Industry* (New York, The Macmillan Co., 1940), pp. 10–11.

and to secure a "safe market and a safe source
of raw materials in China."

China cannot supply rubber and oil, but the
German occupation of Holland and France
and threat to Great Britain afford Japan an opportunity to expand into Indo-China, the
Netherlands East Indies, and possibly Malaya.
The Japanese Navy prefers expansion to the
southeastward to the penetration of China.

According to a news report in November
1940, Admiral Takahashi, former Commander in Chief of Japan's Combined Fleet,
wrote that the "new order in Greater East
Asia" begins with Manchukuo in the north
and extends to Australia in the south, ending
in the east at 180° longitude and extending in
the west to the Bay of Bengal and Burma. "It
will be constructed in several stages. In the
first stage, the sphere that Japan demands
includes Manchukuo, China, Indo-China,
Burma, Straits Settlements, Netherlands Indies, New Caledonia, New Guinea, many
islands in the West Pacific, Japan's mandated
islands and the Philippines. Australia and the
rest of the East Indies can be included later."
"Greater Asia," he said, "will be built up in
proportion to Japan's national strength. The

greater our strength, the larger will be the sphere of Greater East Asia."[8]

Whether Admiral Takahashi made the remarks credited to him matters little. Many other influential Japanese have uttered sentiments of the same tenor; but it is the actions of the Japanese Government, not the words of her officials, that give the best evidence of Japan's future intentions. Japan began a program of expansion within two decades of the abandonment of the policy of exclusion. She has consciously imitated the methods of Russia, Germany and Great Britain. She has become an industrialized nation and her high birth rate provides her with a surplus population to export. Her leaders are sincerely convinced that Japan must expand or perish. Takahashi's statement, then, carries internal evidence of its accuracy. In general any naval officer would agree that a nation's capacity for expansion depends chiefly upon its military strength. A Japanese admiral would not hesitate to express such views, and to inspire his countrymen to greater efforts he could be ex-

8. Hugh Byas, "Japan Said To Ask All of The Orient," *New York Times,* November 14, 1940.

pected to resort to the terse phraseology in the statement, "The greater our strength the larger will be the sphere of Greater East Asia."

In the autumn of 1936 Japan and Germany formed an anti-Comintern pact directed against communism and the Soviet Government; a year later Mussolini was allowed to join. The Japanese Government, surprised by the suddenness of the Hitler-Stalin agreement, in August 1939 scrapped the pact and recovered their freedom of action; on September 27, 1940, Japan rejoined the Axis powers and declared her intention to coöperate with them in establishing a new order in Europe and Asia. Subsequently Japan dispatched a special envoy to Moscow to negotiate a nonaggression pact with the Soviet, and began withdrawing troops from certain localities in China and assembling an expeditionary force on Hainan Island near French Indo-China.

On December 19 Foreign Minister Yosuke Matsuoka warned the United States against joining the European war. He said that "Japan is and will remain loyal to her Allies, that Japan's foreign policy will revolve in the future around the three-power pact and to have any illusion on such an issue would do no good to any one."[9] On that date military and economic commissions were named to implement the new alliance, a move that gave it increased significance.

Berlin and Rome, whose attacks on the United Kingdom and Egypt had not proceeded as advertised, boasted of their new follower. It would have been more correct for them to say that they were following Tokio. If, during the last decade, Americans had watched the Far East as carefully as they did Europe, they would not have been surprised at Japan's defiance of the United States and her announcement that she would fight on the side of the Axis powers if the United States entered the war. Since 1931 when she established a protectorate over Manchuria, and particularly since 1937 when she invaded central China, Japan has shown a conspicuous disregard for American trade, missions, institutions and prestige in the Far East. The fact that Japanese officers bombed the U.S.S. *Panay* and her convoy of merchantmen in broad daylight should convince Americans that important members

9. Hugh Byas, "Matsuoka Pleads for Peace," *ibid.*, December 20, 1940.

of the Japanese military establishment are determined to pursue their national objectives even if it involves risk of war with the United States. The military will leave it to their Foreign Office to present plausible explanations to Washington, but will not be deterred from their program by any formal expressions of American disapproval.

The American people have been fully informed of the purposes of the Japanese Government by His Excellency Hirosi Saito,[10] Ambassador to the United States from 1934 to 1939. Speaking as the official representative of his country's policies, Saito attempted to explain Japan's actions in China and Manchuria; while endeavoring to propitiate American opinion, he frankly warned the United States that his government were resolved to pursue their own deliberately chosen course of action in China.

In 1935 Saito told the Woman's Club at Richmond, Virginia: "Our position in the Far East must be paramount for strategic reasons," as well as for geographic and economic reasons. He explained the occupation of Manchuria by the straightforward statement that it

10. He has since died.

was necessary to establish order there because "in Manchuria Japan has vital interests." The Japanese Foreign Office, he reminded his audience, had officially informed Washington in 1922 that "Japan's position was more important in the Far East than that of any Western nation."[11]

In other addresses Saito emphasized the size of Japanese-American trade, implying that it would be well to let Japan become the overlord of China and dominate the Far East because our trade with Japan would increase. He stressed the point that the United States would not have to maintain gunboats in Japan to protect its trade as was necessary in China. Viscount Ishii used the same argument in 1917 when he endeavored to persuade the United States to let Japan act as broker for the entire American Far Eastern trade.

In spite of Saito's assurances the following instances of discrimination against American trade explain why it has invariably declined in Japanese occupied areas. The purpose of the Manchukuo Exchange Control Law of Octo-

11. Hirosi Saito, *Japan's Policies and Purposes: Selections from Recent Addresses and Writings* (Boston, Marshall Jones Co., 1935), pp. 126, 120, 88.

ber 7, 1937, as formally stated, was "to curtail unnecessary imports from countries other than Japan." Import permits are required for all imports except Japanese. Under the exchange control system enforced by the Manchukuoan puppet government, all transactions in foreign currencies including American dollars are subject to strict control. The Japanese yen is the sole exception.

By a Manchukuoan law of April 10, 1935, the importation and sale of petroleum products other than lubricating oils became a government monopoly. The Manchukuoan Motion Picture Law of 1937 resulted in the withdrawal of all American movie firms and films from Manchuria. January 1, 1938, a new Manchukuo tariff went into effect, with the announced purpose of aiding "the smooth development of Japan-Manchukuoan trade."

The Manchukuo Government has organized a monopoly, owned jointly with a Mr. Aikawa (a Japanese magnate), in the mining of coal and iron, and the manufacture of aircraft and automobiles. The Manshu Tobacco Company has a monopoly of the tobacco business of Manchuria. Commerce in China is directed by Japan through monopolies for the export and import of commodities in areas under the control of Japanese military and naval authorities or of local puppet governments. Discriminatory tariffs are imposed in these areas. By military regulations the Yangtze is practically closed to all commercial shipping except Japanese.

With the exception of the decade when Japan was preparing for her first war with Russia, there has been almost continuous Japanese-American rivalry in the Pacific for fifty years. Exclusion of the Japanese from the United States and the gradual shutting out of American commerce from Japanese-occupied territory in China in violation of the open-door policy were the basic causes of the ill-will that on at least two occasions brought the nations to the verge of war. Mutual forbearance and absorption in other matters preserved the peace.

The two root causes of this hostility still exist and the military situation has become more delicate with the adherence of Japan to the Berlin-Rome Axis. With Great Britain in command of the Atlantic Ocean the United States could concede the military initiative to

Japan in the western Pacific, because the United States Fleet would be stationed in the Pacific and free to operate as long as necessary against Japan without any anxiety for the Atlantic seaboard. And the United States Fleet could reasonably expect to overcome in a short time any initial advantage gained by Japan. If the control of the Atlantic by the British Fleet were seriously threatened, it might become necessary to transfer the fleet to the Atlantic and keep it there for a considerable period of time during which Japan could make herself almost unassailable in the western Pacific. In view of this possibility the American High Command can no longer safely concede the initiative to Japan, and before it transfers the fleet to the Atlantic it will have to take prompt measures to secure the military position of the army in the Philippines.

If the American Fleet were transferred to the Atlantic, Japan would be free to invade Malaya, Australasia or the Philippines. Such action would be in harmony with the program of her navy and army leaders, and in accord with the Clausewitz theory of war as an instrument of policy which should be resorted to under the most favorable circumstances. An attack by Japan on Singapore, Batavia or Manila while the United States Fleet was in the Atlantic would seem to Americans to be a stab in the back. To the Japanese it would simply mean putting into practice precepts they had learned from Christian nations.

In singular contrast to Japan's attitude toward war is the assumption generally made in the United States that wars can usually be avoided by abandoning certain rights, by the failure to exercise some others, or by backing away from each dangerous situation as it arises. As a satisfied power the United States *is* peaceful and so has little understanding of nations that for many reasons are dissatisfied with their boundaries. The American attitude toward war is completely misunderstood in Japan. For instance when the United States withdrew its forces from Vera Cruz in 1914 in accordance with the terms of mediation proposed by Argentina, Brazil and Chile, accounts of the evacuation published in the native Japanese papers implied that the United States was a nation of tradesmen who evacuated Vera Cruz on account of the comparatively small losses suffered in the landing operations. This view was accepted by Japanese editors, who obviously were not acquainted with President Wilson's reasons for withdrawing. A similar lack of understanding of the Japanese attitude toward war exists in the United States, and Americans fancy that a few hotheaded army and naval officers are able to force a reluctant nation to fight aggressive wars for their personal glory and advancement. Actually these officers are influential because they represent the desires of their people to expand.

The basic cause of Japan's desire to obtain more territory is innate and for that reason is more dangerous than if it had been artificially created: it springs from the fecund, virile, courageous and acquisitive Japanese people. Their rapid rise to power is due in no small measure to the wisdom of their leaders of the previous generation who carefully limited the national ambitions to the nation's strength, which in Admiral Takahashi's formula is the only limit of their ambition. But there is some evidence that the present leaders in Japan have overtaxed her powers in the Chinese adventure, and if Japan attempts to dominate the whole Far East, she may overreach herself and burst like the bullfrog that attempted to become as large as an ox.

CHAPTER TWO

JAPANESE MILITARY ORGANIZATION

THE Japanese institutions described in this chapter are frequently compared with corresponding ones in the United States, but it should be emphasized that no Japanese institution is exactly like its American or European counterpart. The customs and manners of orientals and occidentals are entirely unlike, their moral concepts and their standards of conduct are fundamentally different. When the Japanese leaders in the middle of the last century decided to emerge from their seclusion, they knew their people too well to attempt to transplant Western institutions unchanged to Japan; they borrowed some Western ideas, modified them to accord with the characteristics of their own people, and adapted their institutions to conform generally with their Western models. The fundamental difference between modern Japan and other Asi-

atic countries arises from three facts. Japanese
leaders of their own volition decided to modernize Japan. The patriotism and military ca-
pacities of the people furnished the materials
for an army and navy that secured them liberty
to develop naturally in accordance with their
national genius, a privilege which was denied
other Asiatics who opposed innovations but
lacked the military skill to resist aggression.
And in 1889 Emperor Meiji voluntarily be-
stowed a Constitution upon his people, which
with little internal strife transformed a feudal
organization into an efficient highly central-
ized monarchy. It limited his own authority in
certain respects, but sovereignty still belongs
entirely to the Emperor and all power is exercised in his name. Theoretically the Emperor
exercises the legislative power with the consent
of the Imperial Diet, but the Constitution contains the means to obtain that consent. The
Emperor convokes the Diet, opens, closes and
prorogues it, and he can dissolve the House of
Representatives. The Diet must be convoked
once a year, but a session cannot last longer
than three months. In case an emergency
should arise when the Diet is not sitting, the
Emperor may issue ordinances which have the

effect of laws. These become invalid if not approved by the succeeding Diet. Several Japanese statesmen have labored to establish parliamentary government based upon a party system with cabinets responsible to the Diet, but the Imperial Precepts and Ordinances and the Constitution itself have enabled the official bureaucracy, the army and the navy to prevent this innovation.

The Emperor has supreme command of the army and navy, determines their organization and peace standing, can declare a state of siege, a state of war, make peace and conclude treaties. The first Imperial Ordinance concerning the military establishments antedates the Constitution and has equal authority with it. By Imperial decree the army and navy are exempt from any interference by the Diet or the government in all matters of internal organization, composition and regulation.[1]

1. The Imperial Diet is limited in its powers and duration of session. Article V of the Constitution restricts the Diet to giving (or presumably refusing) consent to legislation proposed by the throne. In practice the Diet exercises some initiative in legislation. Changes in the Constitution can be proposed only by the Emperor, and none have been made. See *The Japan Year Book, 1939–1940* (Tokio, The Foreign Affairs Association of Japan), chap. iv, or *1937*, chap. vii.

The army budget is prepared by the Minister of War and the navy budget by the Minister of Marine; each is then submitted to the Minister of the Treasury. The budget for the entire government is submitted to the Diet by the Treasury Department, but the War and Navy Ministers explain and when necessary defend their own estimates in the Diet. If their estimates are not accepted either minister can cause a cabinet crisis by resigning.[2]

A Prime Minister endeavoring to form a cabinet must choose his Minister of War from the generals or lieutenant generals on the active list of the army, and his Minister of Marine from the admirals or vice-admirals on the active list of the navy. High ranking army and naval officers have frequently combined, to prevent a prospective Prime Minister whom they distrusted from forming a cabinet, by refusing to accept office, or forced the reorganization of an unfriendly cabinet by one of their members resigning the military or naval portfolio. Some writers have condemned this con-

2. If the Diet reduces the estimates below the amount necessary to finance the projects outlined by the Ministers of War or Marine, it is deemed to have infringed the Imperial Prerogative under Article XII of the Constitution. *The Japan Year Book, 1939–1940,* p. 209.

duct as unconstitutional, when actually these officers have only exercised their constitutional prerogatives after being convinced that their responsibility to the Emperor for the protection of their country and its interests demanded drastic action.

Each cabinet minister is directly responsible to the Emperor for the conduct and efficiency of his department, and the authority of the Prime Minister over cabinet members is correspondingly lessened. Owing to the privileged status of the army and navy, their ministers seldom hesitate to take an independent attitude toward the Prime Minister. Their example is sometimes followed by army commanders in the field who, if the military exigencies of a situation appear to demand a new course of action, are ready to adopt it even if it establishes a new national policy or modifies an old one. Having made a decision, which may involve other nations and have far-reaching consequences, they will not permit any change in their announced course of action, even by the Foreign Office, asserting that the determination of the military action taken in any military situation is a prerogative of the Imperial Command and no civilian agency can interfere with military decisions. Generals commanding in the field are subordinate to the Chief of the Army General Staff and would loyally follow his directives, but they do not consider themselves necessarily limited by the policies announced by the Foreign Office. And it should be repeated that there is warrant in the Imperial Constitution, Imperial Ordinances, Imperial Precepts, the unwritten law and the customs of Japan to support the actions of the military chiefs.

The navy is less brusque in its manners than the army, but it enjoys the same privileges; when naval interests are threatened, it permits no interference by the Foreign Office. During the negotiations before the last London Conference on the Limitation of Naval Armaments, the Minister of Marine was not pleased with the reaction of American newspapers to the Japanese claim to naval parity with the United States; he ordered a captain of the navy to Washington as spokesman for the department. On his arrival the captain ostentatiously ignored the Ambassador, summoned correspondents to the Embassy, and explained the position the Japanese Government would take at London, requesting them to inform the

American people why the Japanese Navy must have parity with Great Britain and the United States.

From the beginning the Japanese naval officers objected to the Naval Limitations Treaty of 1922. Admiral Baron Kato, head of the Japanese delegation, succeeded in attaching to it a provision that limited fortification of American territory in the Far East. But even Admiral Kato, who had served on the staff of Togo and was known to enjoy his confidence, could not reconcile Japanese officers to naval limitations. Between the naval conferences of 1921 and of 1930, taking full advantage of the failure to limit the construction of cruisers, destroyers and submarines, they concentrated their efforts on building "a powerful fleet of auxiliary ships to compensate for the deficiency in capital ships" permitted to Japan.[3] She completed 20 cruisers, including 8 carrying 8-inch guns, while the United States completed 10 armed only with 6-inch guns. The conference of 1930, largely on the insistence of the United States, extended the limitations to all classes of ships and to gain Japan's consent increased her over-all ratio of 5 to 3 to approximately 10 to

3. *The Japan Year Book, 1937*, p. 241.

7. This did not reduce the resentment of the Japanese Navy. Their attitude was shared by the public, and a number of cabinet officials including two premiers were killed by Japanese chauvinists because of the signing of the treaty.

The naval officers continued dissatisfied and in 1934, during the preliminary discussion of the agenda for the next conference, put forward in the name of the Japanese Government an entirely new formula for limitations based upon:

1. The total abolition of aircraft carriers and capital ships.

2. The fixing of a common maximum limit for the naval strengths to be held by the powers concerned.

3. The common maximum limit to be as low as possible.[4]

Adoption of these three provisions undoubtedly would have advanced the cause of naval disarmament, but it would have done much more. Abolition of aircraft carriers and capital ships would have increased the relative naval strength of Japan by eliminating the two

4. Saito, *Japan's Policies and Purposes: Selections from Recent Addresses and Writings*, p. 8.

classes in which she was weaker and which were less necessary to support her naval policies; it would have left untouched her cruisers, in which she had achieved actual superiority over the United States. Fixing a common maximum limit for all nations would have conceded her claim to parity, for which she had been contending in vain since 1922. Most important, a low maximum limit on all naval strength would have made it impossible for Great Britain or the United States to exercise any influence in the western Pacific, and would have left Japan with sufficient naval force to control all eastern Asiatic waters. In spite of the disingenuousness of the proposal, Ambassador Saito solemnly offered it to the American people in two public addresses as a plan "conceived with a genuine desire to advance the work of disarmament."[5]

In January 1936 the Japanese delegation withdrew from the London Naval Conference and virtually ended all hope of further naval limitation. American naval officers also opposed the principle of naval limitation on the ground that armament was the result of national rivalries, and that it was useless there-

5. *Ibid.*, p. 7.

fore to attempt naval limitation until nations would limit their ambitions. Japanese naval officers were able to influence both the Japanese Government and Japanese public opinion; American naval officers had little influence either in the government or on the American public.

It is sometimes difficult for foreign officials to reconcile statements made by official spokesmen of three different Japanese departments, State, War and Navy, each of which has constitutional authority to speak; but the Japanese system has some advantages. Usually the Ministers of Foreign Affairs, War and Navy agree upon a course of action, the Emperor gives his assent, and all the energy in Japan is concentrated upon the undertaking. Frequently the premier is an admiral or a general, and usually he is imbued with the doctrine of Clausewitz that "war is a real political instrument, . . . an act of violence intended to compel an opponent to fulfill our will."

In 1872, when the Japanese Government determined to modernize their armed forces on occidental lines, they modeled their army first after the French, then after the German, and their navy after the British. They sent young army officers to Germany and young naval officers to England to study methods and organization. Soon thereafter they established their own military and naval academies in Japan, employing German and British instructors reënforced by the Japanese officers who had studied abroad. These elementary academies were later supplemented by postgraduate schools and war colleges.

The United States Navy assisted in the modernization of Japan's fleet. Japanese midshipmen were entered at our Naval Academy, several of whom subsequently distinguished themselves. A notable example was Naval Cadet Sotokichi Uriu, who was graduated with the class of 1881 and commanded a division of cruisers under Togo during the Russo-Japanese War. His division took a leading part in the opening engagements of the war, protected the landing of Japanese troops in Chemulpo Harbor, Korea, and afterward forced the Russian cruiser *Variag* and gunboat *Korietz* to scuttle themselves in harbor to avoid destruction or capture.

Today Japan has three naval academies to train midshipmen for their future duties as ensigns; the first located at Etajima near Kure in the Inland Sea, for those aspiring to the command or executive branch; the second at Maizuru for those preparing for engineering duties; the third at Tokio for those qualifying themselves for assistant paymasters. Naval constructors are educated at civil universities; after a professional examination they enter the navy with the rank of junior lieutenant. The Naval War College at Tokio is somewhat similar to the American but devotes more time to preparing its students, usually lieutenant commanders, for staff duties than for high command.

The enlisted personnel of the navy is about 60 per cent volunteers and 40 per cent conscripts. The proportion varies but service in the navy is popular and many volunteer although the term of enlistment is six years, while a naval conscript is required to serve only three. Most of the petty officers are volunteers who have reënlisted and propose to make the navy a life career. Recruits receive their elementary training ashore, by the same methods used in the United States. They are taught to take care of their persons and their own belongings, and are given much infantry drill. Recruit training usually continues for six months before the men are ordered to a sea-going ship of the fleet.

The personnel of the navy includes at least four detachments of "Sea Infantry" similar in some respects to our Marine Corps. Units of the Sea Infantry are stationed ashore at each of the four naval districts; they are commanded by regular naval officers who serve on this duty ashore four years and train their men as a "landing force" of infantry. When necessary to effect a landing on a hostile shore, the Sea Infantry may be a covering force for a large landing party of which the army will provide the main body; or when small opposition is anticipated, the Sea Infantry will undertake a landing without reënforcement from the army.

The Japanese Military Academy at Tokio offers a four-year course similar to that at West Point to cadets who are commissioned second lieutenants on graduation. There are also post-graduate schools and the Army War College, but the latter like the Naval War College devotes more time to the preparation of officers for duty on the General Staff than for high command. In this respect it resembles our

Command and General Staff School more than our Army War College at Washington.

Since 1872 Japan has manned her armies and fleets by conscription. An army conscript serves two years in the Active Army (*Gen-eki*) and five years in the Active Army Reserve (*Yobi-eki*), during which he is recalled to the colors for an annual refresher training course of from two to six weeks. He then passes into the Reserve Army (*Kobi hei-eki*), where he is not required to take annual training, and finally into the Territorial Army (*Kokumin hei-eki*), where he is liable for service in any national emergency until he is forty years old. Army conscripts are trained for a particular branch such as artillery or infantry for two years, but special artificer ratings such as tank mechanics are given longer periods of training.

Officers of the army and navy are well trained, zealous in the performance of duty and have proven their courage on many occasions. They are patriotic, frequently chauvinistic, strict disciplinarians but with an almost parental concern for the welfare of their men.

The revolt of young army officers on February 26, 1936, resulted from their feeling of responsibility for the welfare of their men, which made them responsive to suggestions from former army officers who were actuated by different motives. For several years conditions in rural Japan had been steadily getting worse due to the maladjustment between agriculture and industry; disparity between prices and wages was intensified by the boom in the munitions industry incident to the preparations for war in China in 1937. The industrial workers were able to get higher wages to compensate for the increase in the cost of living; the farm laborers had no redress and their families felt the full force of the inflation. Regimental and company officers learned from their own privates, who came from peasant families, of the deplorable conditions in the homes of the farmers, and were better informed of internal conditions than many members of the Diet. They determined that these conditions among the peasantry and the small country gentry which furnish many of the officers must be improved.

Usually junior officers are loyal and subordinate to higher authority but on this occasion they allowed themselves to be convinced that these unhealthy conditions existed because the

Emperor was being badly advised by his ministers and some of the senior officers of the army and navy. The junior officers have an association formed for professional improvement. Disappointed in the Liberal victory in the February elections, which meant curtailment of military appropriations, they determined to rid the Emperor of his evil councilors by assassination. Viscount Saito and Finance Minister Takahashi were murdered; other intended victims narrowly escaped.

The Army High Command, realizing that their junior officers were inspired by a genuine desire to improve the lives of the peasantry, parleyed with the rebels before taking extreme measures. The Navy High Command, deeply concerned over the revolt, sent detachments of Sea Infantry from Yokosuka Naval Station to protect their officers on duty in Tokio, and it is reported that when the army leaders delayed taking drastic measures against the mutineers, the navy informed them that if the army could not restore order in the nation's capital the navy would. After the army suppressed the mutiny, seventeen of the ringleaders of the revolt were executed and others were impris-

oned. Soon thereafter the new ministry insti-
tuted reforms designed to improve the conditions in agrarian Japan.

The fleet and naval establishments ashore
are constructed, maintained and operated under the supervision of three admirals stationed
in Tokio, each of whom has complete authority and corresponding responsibility within his
own sphere.

The Chief of the Technical Division was ap-
pointed and his division created to meet the
situation peculiar to Japan, which depends
upon the rapid and skilful adaptation of foreign naval improvements more than upon the
developments made in the factories and labo-
ratories in Japan. There is no corresponding
official in the navy departments of other countries. His primary duty is to make certain that
Japanese ships and naval materials, including
naval aviation, are equal to any produced
abroad. For this purpose he maintains in Europe and the United States numerous assistants who watch all technical developments in
naval and aviation material, and buy samples
of all new naval instruments. When these are
sent to Tokio they are compared with similar

Japanese products. Any superior features of the foreign instruments are embodied in the next Japanese design if practicable; otherwise a license is obtained to manufacture them at home or they are ordered from abroad.

In addition the Chief of the Technical Division is responsible to the Emperor for the construction of all naval vessels in Japan, including the hulls, machinery, armor and armament, and he must see that all naval material meets the required specifications. He has assistants for these duties who regularly inspect naval material and ships building at home. Until recently the chief of this division was chosen from the naval constructors; but when a small torpedo boat capsized due to faulty design the division was reorganized and placed under an admiral of the line, who has constructors and engineers among his assistants. The army does not have a corresponding bureau but it also maintains a large number of attachés abroad to report improvements in arms and equipment, and is well informed of modern military implements. Lack of money has prevented the army from adopting the motorized equipment of European armies. Army leaders have made a virtue of necessity and boast that the Japanese travel light and do not need the elaborate transport system of the Europeans.

The Minister of Marine provides the personnel to man the ships when they are completed, furnishes necessary stores and equipment, and thereafter is responsible for the continuous supply of personnel and the maintenance of the material.

The Chief of the Naval Staff is responsible for the operation, mobilization and intelligence duties of the navy—that is, he is responsible for the preparations of the fleet for war. He has direct authority over the Commander in Chief of the Combined Fleet and the commandants of the four naval districts in all that concerns operations of the fleets and shore establishments.

These three officers coöperate closely. Ordinarily they execute their functions through the commandants of the naval districts, whose organizations provide the officers to supervise and control all shore operations. In addition the Chief of the General Staff supervises the operations and training schedules of the fleet through the Commander in Chief. The chain of command in the fleet follows the established practices in the British and American Navies, with much less discretion extended to the Commander in Chief afloat than is usual in the United States Navy.

Japanese aviation is an integral part of the fleet and army, as it is in the United States; Japan has developed aircraft carriers for her fleet following the example of Great Britain and the United States. She could afford to offer to scrap them in 1934, however, if other nations followed suit, because with her chain of islands she could base her naval aircraft ashore, conveniently placed to coöperate with her fleet in the Far East, while the United States, which has failed to develop bases in that area, is more dependent on carrier-based planes.

The Chief of the Technical Division, the Minister of Marine, the Chief of the Navy General Staff, and the Commander in Chief of the Combined Fleet each has direct access to the Emperor and the right of appeal from a proposed course of action he considers harmful to the navy or the nation.[6] Since no Em-

6. In this respect the organization of the Japanese Navy Department resembles that of the German Navy under Emperor William II, when the Minister of Marine, the Chief of the Navy General Staff or the Commander of the High Seas Fleet could appeal directly to the Emperor.

peror could be expected to decide difficult technical questions when carefully trained patriotic officers cannot agree upon a solution, serious disagreements between high naval officials are referred to the Superior Naval Council, composed of elder naval statesmen. Officers who cannot reconcile themselves to the proposed action quietly resign, and their successors join with those in office in submitting a unanimous recommendation to the Emperor.

The Commander in Chief of the Combined Fleet has much the same duties as the Commander in Chief of the United States Pacific Fleet; he is usually in immediate command of the First Fleet, to which the Second Fleet is joined annually for naval maneuvers. In addition to these two fleets, there are naval district forces that are assigned to the four districts in Japan, and others assigned to overseas districts, notably in Formosa and the Caroline and Marshall Islands. At present there are considerable naval forces operating in China in support of the army. These are organized into the First and Second Fleets in Chinese waters, and each fleet has its own commander in chief.

The Japanese Navy uses the term commander in chief more frequently than the United States Navy, which has only three Commanders in Chief. The authority of the Commander in Chief of the Combined Fleet is not as extensive as that of the Commander in Chief, United States Pacific Fleet, and he is not allowed the same initiative by his Chief of General Staff, who issues very specific training directives, strictly supervises all fleet exercises, and maintains close control over the dispositions and movements of the fleet by issuing operation orders in great detail.

The Japanese Army has its own Superior Council, or court of last resort, similar in all respects to that of the navy. In spite of all these agencies, occasionally truculent, strong-willed admirals or generals refuse to be reconciled or silenced until admonished by the Emperor to end a controversy; but in the great majority of cases these two Superior Councils can control the officers of both services.

The Army and Navy Superior Councils unite to form the Supreme War Council, which is practically an Army-Navy Privy Council to the Emperor, under whose authority it determines all joint policies affecting the services. It is frequently requested by the Emperor to determine policies which in the United States would be fixed by the President and the Secretary of State. After the major army-navy policies have been decided in principle by the Supreme War Council, the common objectives are accomplished by an exchange of staff officers between the two services who maintain the necessary liaison and supervise the execution of the combined operations.

The Japanese Army, modeled after the German, has a General Staff to operate, and a Minister of War to provide, the men and materials. The army is organized into companies, battalions, regiments, brigades, divisions and armies. Divisions are based upon definite geographical regions known as division areas. A battalion of infantry numbering about 1,000 men is the normal combat unit and operates under the immediate command of its major or lieutenant colonel. A division consists of 2 infantry brigades (equal to 4 regiments or 12 battalions), 1 cavalry regiment, 1 artillery regiment, 1 engineer battalion, with field and bridging units, and technical and special service troops such as the signal corps, totaling about 15,000 troops. A unit often employed in the field is a mixed or reënforced brigade which approximates in strength half a division.

The tendency in European armies is to reduce the number of infantrymen in each company, which correspondingly reduces the number of men in all higher echelons. This reduction is accomplished without corresponding loss in fire power, by supplying automatic rifles and machine guns in place of the ordinary rifle. Japanese equipment lags behind European and is counterbalanced by an increased number of infantrymen. Today European divisions average less than 15,000 troops; in Japan the number is higher, but is likely to decrease as Japan rearms.

Despite the Supreme War Council unanimity of army-navy opinion is often difficult to obtain. It is known that the Japanese Army has favored a deeper penetration into the continent of Asia, while the navy would prefer to expand seaward along the chain of islands leading into Malaya; both agree that expansion in some direction is a national necessity. Japanese newspapers have published statements that the navy has warned the army against becoming heavily involved in Asia before the fleet is prepared to guarantee its sea communications against external attack by a superior fleet.

Army and navy have coöperated very cordially in joint operations both in the highest echelons where the general plans are made and in actual tactical operations such as a joint landing on a hostile shore. The admiral commanding the squadron supporting the landing is in command of the entire operation until the covering force of Sea Infantry has captured the first objectives; he also retains command if compelled to withdraw or abandon the enterprise. The second wave, composed of army troops specially trained for landing operations, follows closely behind the Sea Infantry, to enlarge their holdings, and particularly to secure docks, wharves and adjacent port facilities that will expedite the landing of the main body of the army and permit transports and supply ships to berth alongside docks and discharge their troops and material. When the army has been landed in such force that it can advance or successfully maintain itself against the enemy, command ashore passes to it. The naval commander will remain responsible for securing the army's sea communications and providing the necessary supplies. This common-sense system has been employed successfully throughout the recent war in China.

A foreigner might easily consider the organization of the Japanese Army, Navy and cabinet as cumbersome, overlapping, bureaucratic and top heavy. Before accepting such a conclusion it would be well to examine the operations of a similar organization before and during the war with Russia in 1904–5.

In 1896 the Japanese leaders and people were convinced that they had been robbed of their victory over China by the concerted action of Russia, Germany and France. When Russia occupied Port Arthur and the Liaotung Peninsula which, in coöperation with France and Germany, she had forced Japan to restore to China, Japan began preparations for a war that would gain control of Korea, eject Russia from Manchuria and establish Japan as the dominant power there.

In her preparations Japan followed exactly the system suggested by Karl von Clausewitz in his book on war. The Ministers of War and Navy estimated the forces necessary to defeat the Russian Army and Navy in the Far East, the Minister of Finance calculated the total cost and recommended sources of revenue. The entire government united their efforts in reconciling the people to new taxes by directing public indignation against Russia for robbing Japan of Port Arthur.

The skill and determination shown by successive Japanese ministries in preparing for this war are described clearly by Col. E. L. V. Cordonnier, of the French Army, at one time Commander of the 119th Infantry Regiment and Professor at the École Supérieure de Guerre, who was attached to the Russian Armies during the Manchurian campaign.[7] As a representative of an allied army he was given an opportunity to witness the events of the war. At the École Supérieure de Guerre he had further opportunity to study the entire development of Russo-Japanese relations from 1896 to 1905 when Japan defeated Russia. In the second chapter of his book, Colonel Cordonnier establishes the complete identity of the measures advocated by Clausewitz with those followed by the State, War and Navy Departments of Japan in preparing for and prosecut-

7. See E. L. V. Cordonnier, *The Japanese in Manchuria, 1904* (London, Hugh Rees, 1912). Translated by C. F. Atkinson.

ing the war with Russia. Cordonnier is corroborated by testimony from the Japanese High Command itself. In 1885 Major Meckel, of the German Army, who had been a student of Moltke, went to Japan at the head of a military mission to instruct the Japanese Army in European methods of war and remained several years. After the battle of Liao-Yang, Marshal Oyama cabled General (the former Major) Meckel, "We hope you are proud of your pupils." In response to a direct question concerning this telegram asked by Maj. Stewart L. Murray of the Gordon Highlanders, author of *The Reality of War,* General Meckel said, "I, like every other German officer, have consciously or unconsciously instructed in the spirit of Clausewitz." The final bit of evidence comes from the war correspondent of the London *Times,* who was with the Japanese Army. In his book, *The War in the Far East,* he stated: "All save one of the great battles in Manchuria have been waged by the Japanese in close accordance with the spirit and almost the letter of Clausewitz's doctrines."[8] From the day the Japanese Government determined to

8. Military Correspondent of *The Times, The War in the Far East, 1904–1905* (London, John Murray, 1905), p. 550.

avenge themselves on the Russians for their expulsion from Port Arthur until the peace of Portsmouth in 1905, the Japanese military hierarchy followed chapter by chapter the advice given by Clausewitz. This may have been a coincidence, but Cordonnier, a French Army officer, did not think so, the London *Times* military correspondent did not think so, and Marshal Oyama handsomely acknowledged his obligations to General Meckel, who formally stated that not only he but every other German officer instructed in "the spirit of Clausewitz."[9]

Even skilfully raised, the increased taxation required under the Clausewitz doctrine provoked more than one riot among the populace and caused the downfall of four cabinets within three years. Each succeeding government persevered; the money they wrung from their comparatively poor population was honestly and efficiently expended. The army and navy grew steadily stronger, Japan's value as an ally increased, and on January 30, 1902, she was admitted to full partnership with

9. The same is true of Mahan and naval war. Time and again at the Naval War College and in papers on naval subjects, writers and lecturers have consciously or unconsciously repeated the teaching of Mahan.

Great Britain, while she was being wooed by Russia.

The alliance with England alarmed Russia, and in answer to Japanese protests she promised to evacuate Manchuria but never fulfilled her engagements. By the summer of 1903 the Japanese Army was ready. The Navy lagged behind: the battle line of 6 battleships and 8 armored cruisers was a little more than half the total Russian strength; but almost half the Russian Fleet was in the Baltic. By striking quickly Japan could secure local and temporary control of the sea in the strategic area of operations. Her own fleet, commanded by Vice-Admiral Togo, was concentrated and favorably disposed to strike the first blow.

The time of the attack was hastened by a report that the Russians were about to reënforce their Port Arthur Squadron, which would have made it numerically superior to the Japanese Fleet. Two Japanese cruisers recently bought from Argentina were still at Singapore and might be intercepted en route to Japan; it was a critical time. Above all, it was essential to strike the Russian Fleet before it was reënforced from the Baltic. An ultimatum was delivered to St. Petersburg on January 13, the Ambassador recalled on February 6, and three days later without a formal declaration of war Togo's destroyers made their first attack on the unguarded Russian ships at Port Arthur.

The Japanese High Command realized that to win they must defeat the Russians at sea and in Manchuria. Togo boldly accepted the risk of covering the army landing in Korea and Manchuria and protecting its communications by blockading the undefeated Russian Fleet in Port Arthur. In a loyal effort to assist Togo General Nogi repeatedly attacked Port Arthur to compel the Russian Fleet to leave the protection of the forts and give Togo an opportunity to destroy it at sea. The Russian squadron made two brief sorties but Togo did not succeed in destroying it. Meanwhile Rojestvensky was en route with the entire Baltic Fleet, which might regain control of the sea if it arrived in time to reënforce the fleet at Port Arthur.

Togo again called upon Nogi, who renewed his costly frontal attacks on "203-Meter Hill," took it and forced the surrender of Port Arthur and the remnants of the Russian Far Eastern Squadron on January 2, 1905. Togo was granted almost five months to repair and refit his fleet before Rojestvensky's arrival. With his veteran crews rested and his ships refitted, Togo had no difficulty in destroying the second Russian Fleet in the Sea of Japan on May 27 and 28, and with it went the last hope of Russian victory. Nogi's indomitable infantry who doggedly assaulted Port Arthur contributed equally with Togo's crews to this crowning victory of Japan; and the Japanese cabinets which persevered for a decade in the preparations for war at their own political and personal risk contributed most of all by inspiring the Japanese people to undergo the personal sacrifices which made the victory possible.

CHAPTER THREE

THE AMERICAN HIGH COMMAND

THE majority of the delegates to the Constitutional Convention in Philadelphia were familiar with the futile efforts of the Continental Congress to convert some of its standing committees into efficient executive departments competent to direct the operations of the Continental Navy and Army. Some of these delegates had been members of the Continental Congress that had fled from Philadelphia after conferring wide powers on Gen. George Washington to carry on the war, and they provided in the Constitution of the United States ample authority for the chief executive to wage war, they made the President Commander in Chief of the Army and Navy. Since the Constitution was adopted, and particularly during the Civil War and the years 1917–18, Congress has conferred additional statutory powers upon the chief executive. American war Presidents, notably Lincoln and Wilson, established precedents which were not challenged by the Supreme Court and added still more authority to the chief magistrate.

The Prime Minister of the United Kingdom is only the first among his cabinet colleagues, he must continually persuade them of the soundness of his decisions. The President of the United States selects and dismisses members of his cabinet, they must loyally execute his decisions or resign. The entire British Government may be compelled to resign on short notice by an adverse vote in Parliament; the President, elected for a definite term, can, if the military situation demands, resist public opinion for a time.

For example, the deaths from influenza among American troops on transports bound for France in 1918 were numerous. President Wilson was deluged with letters and telegrams suggesting, even demanding, the suspension of sailings of convoys until the epidemic had abated. He consulted the Chief of the General Staff, Gen. P. C. March, who advised that if the flow of troops to France was halted the war would be prolonged and the total loss of life from sickness and battle before victory could be achieved would be greater. The President realized the validity of March's arguments and ignored the public pressure.[1] Under similar circumstances a Prime Minister of the United Kingdom might have been compelled to bow to public or parliamentary opinion. The war experience of the delegates to the Constitutional Convention, the added grants of power by successive war Congresses, the reluctance of the Federal courts to hamper the executive branch of the government during war, and the initiative of some American war Presidents have combined to create and increase the powers of the presidency until they are for all practical purposes equivalent to those attached to the Imperial crown of Japan.

The President usually delegates his strictly military powers to two civilian cabinet ministers, the Secretary of War and the Secretary of the Navy, whose senior professional advisers are respectively the Chief of Staff of the Army and the Chief of Naval Operations.[2] During war and periods of crisis Presidents often con-

1. Gen. P. C. March, U.S.A., *The Nation at War* (Garden City, N. Y., Doubleday, Doran & Co., 1932), pp. 359–360.
2. See Appendix, p. 261.

sult the military and naval chiefs directly. Cooperation in professional matters between the
two armed services is secured by means of the
Joint Army and Navy Board composed of the
two Secretaries, the Chief of Naval Operations, the Chief of Staff, and their chiefs of war
plans. This is the highest military board in the
United States; if it cannot reach an agreement
on any problem involving both the army and
navy two briefs are submitted to the President,
who as Commander in Chief of the Army and
Navy renders the final decision. Subordinate
to the Joint Army and Navy Board are several
other joint boards, including ones for aeronautics, ordnance and radio. The members of
the Joint Board are assisted by a joint planning
committee, which serves as a permanent secre-
tariat for the Joint Board; this committee
makes preliminary studies and surveys, inves-
tigates proposed plans of action and submits
its findings to the Joint Board, which accepts,
rejects or modifies the recommendations. The
subsidiary boards derive their authority from
the Joint Board and provide the necessary cooperation between similar activities of the
army and navy.

The Joint Board, unlike the Japanese Supreme War Council, is not usually invited to discuss matters of foreign policy, which are regarded as the exclusive concern of the State Department, until hostilities are considered possible or imminent. Then its opinion is sometimes requested on the possible military consequences of State Department policies. During some critical occasions in our history the State Department has not kept the War and Navy Departments informed of developments abroad that might have led to war. The extremely favorable military position of the United States has permitted the State Department to follow this course without serious consequences to the country; but it has more than once prevented the Navy Department or commanders afloat from taking precautionary measures during periods of crisis, disarranged the plans of the navy and jeopardized ships on distant stations. In 1913 two armored cruisers were in the eastern Mediterranean at the time of the Japanese-American tension: the Navy Department wished to order these ships to their war station but was informed that any changes in the disposition of men-of-war might prejudice the negotiations with Tokio. The Japanese Foreign Office offered no objections to the plans of their Navy Department and if hostilities had resulted the Japanese would have enjoyed an initial naval advantage.

The theory that diplomacy alone is sufficient to preserve the peace is as much in error as the assumption that military factors alone are decisive. Government officials charged with formulating national policies and those responsible for the preparations of the armed forces to support these policies should be in close coöperation during peace and war. In peace they should see to it that the country does not embark upon a war that it is not prepared to wage; in war they should make sure that each disposition of the armed forces and every battle fought is directed toward accomplishing the objectives of the government. In the United States the army and navy may not be consulted until the emergency is urgent; in Japan the military are able to overbear the diplomats. In 1914 action by the Russian Foreign Office was precipitated by the rigidity of the army mobilization plan which did not provide for a partial mobilization. To mobilize against Austria it was necessary to order the mobilization of the entire Russian Army which when completed would have placed strong forces of the Russian Army on the German eastern frontiers. The German High Command regarded the mobilization of these forces as a menace to East Prussia, which in fact it would have been, and ordered the mobilization of the German Army.

Whether the mobilization of the Russian Army did actually cause the last war is arguable, but the mobilization plan of any army and the dispositions of the navy should be sufficiently flexible to permit the diplomats to explore all avenues to peace before resorting to war. Diplomats are under a corresponding obligation to the leaders of the army or navy, whom they must keep continuously informed of any policies that might involve the nation in war.

The American War and Navy Departments have never believed that diplomatic negotiations can always settle international disputes. Both departments make assumptions of possible developments in foreign affairs that might lead to hostilities and with these assumptions as a background deduce the political objectives if certain possible wars occur. The best initial dispositions of the army and navy to attain these political objectives are next sought.

The solutions reached become the basis of hypothetical plans.

Until the recent war in Europe upset the balance of power, American military policy was based on "a navy second to none," which would be a shield for the United States and its possessions until the skeletonized regular army filled its cadres. With this initial assumption any American campaign required close coöperation between the army and navy. And the most important function of the Joint Army and Navy Board is to determine the general directives of probable campaigns and to agree upon the measures to be taken by each service. After agreement is reached each chief is responsible for his department's being prepared for its task and both chiefs are responsible for establishing and maintaining the necessary liaison.

By introducing fictional backgrounds the army and navy are able to prepare basic plans for conjectural campaigns. One of these includes an assumption involving the maximum possible national effort, which enables the two departments to prepare plans for their greatest tasks. Reports of military and naval attachés inform the departments of changes abroad that frequently require changes in American plans. By continuously revising their hypothetical plans against imaginary enemies, the army and navy can state at any time their requirements for any specific war that occurs, and as a result of years of joint planning and coöperation they are prepared to make the initial dispositions of their forces for almost any possible war. Thereafter future movements of the fleet and army would depend upon the results of contacts and engagements with enemy forces.

Both the army and navy are convinced that it would be highly dangerous for either department to issue detailed orders to commanders operating thousands of miles away; departmental orders usually outline the military or naval objective and leave the methods of attaining it to be determined by the commander in the field or at sea. The Commander in Chief of the United States Fleet has almost unlimited discretion concerning the means employed during a naval campaign. The practice of the United States Navy differs widely from that of the Japanese where the Naval Chief of Staff in Tokio issues very specific orders to the Commander in Chief of the Combined Fleet, who might disregard directives given by the

Foreign Office but will loyally execute the orders received from the Chief of the Naval General Staff.

The British method of planning for war is more formal and systematic than the American. During his premiership Balfour created the Committee of Imperial Defense for Great Britain, composed primarily of career men from the Foreign Office, which indicates the possible enemies; army, navy and air representatives who calculate the forces necessary to overcome the enemy resistance; and treasury representatives who figure the taxes needed. As occasion requires, representatives of trade, agriculture, industry and labor are temporarily added to the committee. The Prime Minister of the United Kingdom is chairman, and the Prime Ministers of the Dominions are members ex-officio. India is also represented on this imperial committee. MacDonald, Baldwin, and Chamberlain had the mechanism required to prepare Great Britain for war; they simply failed to use it. The United States has no such committee; and while the President has more complete authority than the Prime Minister, he is under the necessity of improvising various national committees in every period of national crisis, with inevitable delay and friction. Except for this deficiency the governmental organization of the United States in its highest echelons is well adapted for the direction, conduct and support of war.

The Joint Munitions Board is not subordinate to the Joint Board; it is headed by an Assistant Secretary of War and an Assistant Secretary of the Navy; its membership includes the chiefs of Naval and Army Ordnance Bureaus. This board performs in time of peace the duties undertaken by the War Industries Board of 1917–18. It estimates in peacetime the material requirements of the army and navy for certain assumed campaigns in the Atlantic or Pacific; it is organized to work in conjunction with a War Industries Board or a similar board in time of war. On the outbreak of war the Joint Munitions Board would be able to furnish to any government agency the requirements of the army and navy and the order of priority of manufactures for them. The War Industries Board or a similar board with a knowledge of industrial facilities would allocate these orders to the plants best fitted to fill them. In theory the Joint Munitions Board simply would have to state its requirements, and a special government agency would meet them. In practice, demand usually exceeds supply, a system of priorities must be established, and factories producing consumer goods diverted to army and navy needs until new factories are built to meet the increased demand.

The Secretary of War and the Secretary of the Navy are personal appointees of the President and immediately responsive to his wishes, but the two departments are in some respects poorly organized, and when the two Secretaries begin to execute presidential orders organizational difficulties appear. The army under the leadership of Theodore Roosevelt and Elihu Root adopted the General Staff system. Theodore Roosevelt attempted to establish a naval General Staff also but the opposition of naval chiefs of bureaus, particularly those of the material bureaus who feared that their almost independent authority would be curbed, assisted by senators and representatives, was strong enough to defeat the necessary legislation in Congress.

In a letter to Theodore Roosevelt written early in 1909, Captain Alfred Thayer Mahan gave his reasons for advocating a General Staff for the navy. They are still valid and worth repeating: "Ideally, the President does and the Secretary [of the Navy], as his lieutenant should, hold in his hands a complete mastery of the diplomatic, military and naval considerations, home and foreign, which for the time being at any given moment affect the policy of the country," for "diplomatic conditions affect military action, and military considerations diplomatic measures. They are inseparable parts of a whole; and as such those responsible for military measures should understand the diplomatic factors, and vice versa." A General Staff "continuous in existence and gradual in change" is the only instrument that will enable the President through the two Secretaries to exercise intelligent control of the navy and the army. At the head of each staff would be a chief who would have the sole responsibility for advising each Secretary and the President, for advice must be individual and weighted with personal responsibility. And these two Chiefs of Staff should be kept informed of the relations existing between our government and other states; with this information on foreign affairs, they become invaluable assistants to their respective chiefs and the President.

The Chief of the Naval Staff would also co-ordinate the administrative work of that department which an incoming civilian Secretary, being unacquainted with the naval and frequently with the business side of the navy, would be unable to do. Mahan did not quarrel with the naval bureaus as such; he thought their necessary but somewhat exaggerated independence should be checked. The Secretary had no agency which would enable him to control and coördinate their activities; this a General Staff could do, and thereby insure that the activities of the various bureaus were all directed toward the same end, the preparation of the fleet for war.

So great is the volume of work and so broad its variety that both the Army and Navy Departments are decentralized into subdivisions known as arms, services and bureaus. Each of these units is efficiently organized on the principle that attaches responsibility to authority and brings poor judgment and incompetence to account. Since it occasionally happens that a chief of one of these subdivisions may regard his bureau as an independent agency and not a cog in the machine, it is clear that a civilian Navy or Army Secretary without military experience or technical knowledge might find it impossible to coördinate the bureaus, arms and services. For this reason the Secretary of War is assisted by the General Staff of the War Department, an organization that enables the Secretary to coördinate and control every action of the immense department, its forces and agencies in the continental United States, its garrisons beyond the seas and the American field armies when and if they are created. In the Navy Department the Chief of Naval Operations has less authority than the Army Chief of Staff and must obtain the coöperation of the chiefs of the various bureaus by suasion.

Since 1918 it has been the policy of the United States to maintain a large navy and a small protective force composed of the Regular Army and the National Guard, both of which could be quickly expanded in an emergency. For the present crisis Congress has appropriated a good deal of money for a two-ocean navy, has adopted conscription to increase the Regular Army and has authorized the President to include the National Guard in the National Army. This expansion of the army and navy has been accompanied by an insistence upon modern armament and equip-

ment and a modification of tactical formations
and methods of training as a result of lessons
learned from the Spanish Civil War and the
present European war.

Army and navy officers will never find themselves in complete agreement on the relative
value of forts versus ships, airplanes versus battleships; naval officers will never agree among
themselves on the relative merits of battleships, destroyers and submarines; nor will
army officers ever reach an agreement on the
relative value of infantry, cavalry or artillery,
or the superior advantages of motorized or
horse-drawn weapons. In such matters there
will always be honest differences of opinion.
There will also be exasperating but probably
not serious delay in executing the present expansion program; for, obviously, the training
of new men, the production of new weapons,
the construction of shelters and the development of training areas cannot be hastily improvised. Time is essential. The War and
Navy Departments are so organized in times
of peace as to facilitate expansion in times of
war. Organizations need to be enlarged only,
not essentially changed; for responsible officers in both services know the needs in men,

ships and material and have carefully arranged programs for obtaining them. Events abroad may compel the navy, and perhaps the army, to take action before preparations are completed to the last button. Even for that sudden crisis there is sufficient flexibility in both organizations to meet the demands made upon them.

There will be little if any confusion within the High Command of the army and navy, who profited by their experience in the last war and are consequently much better prepared than in 1917. Both branches of the military now have their Reserve Officers' Training Corps. These bodies were created in order to avoid the difficulty of the United States in the last war, namely, in obtaining enough trained junior officers for the navy and army.

The various arms and services of the army are directed in accordance with policies prescribed by the War Council, which is composed of the Secretary of War, the Undersecretary of War (formerly the Assistant Secretary of War), and the Chief of Staff. Immediately under the War Council is the General Council, which functions under the Chief of Staff and has in its membership the deputy chief of staff, the five assistant chiefs of staff, and the executive officer of the Undersecretary of War. As the reviewing agency of the department it studies all questions, decides matters of current policy on the basis of principles established by the War Council, and determines what is of sufficient importance to be submitted to the higher authority of the War Council.

In time of emergency or of war, the Regular Army, the National Guard, and the Organized Reserves combine to form the National Army. The Organized Reserves consist mainly of officers. The Regular Army and the National Guard are organized in arms and services. The arms in general do the fighting and consist of Infantry, Cavalry, Field Artillery, Coast Artillery, the Air Corps, the Signal Corps, and the Corps of Engineers. Each of these agencies has in the War Department a chief who is responsible for the elementary training of the troops. The services, on the other hand, include the Adjutant General's Department, the Quartermaster Corps, the Finance Department, the Medical Department, the Ordnance Department, the Chemical Warfare Service and the Corps of Chaplains. Their functions are to supply food, clothing, weapons, ammunition, transportation, and to serve the medical and spiritual needs of the soldiers. Units of some of the services are habitually in the combat zone, where they are exposed to all the dangers of battle without sharing in the exhilaration of fighting.[3]

The National Defense Act of 1920 provides that the Chief of Staff of the Army shall submit his resignation when there is a change of administration. This regulation enables an incoming President to appoint as Chief of Staff the man he believes best suited to prepare the army for war and to prepare himself for the command of the field army by familiarizing himself with the nation's foreign policies, with the measures that will support them, and with the military means that will enforce them. The act also provides that the Chief of Staff shall command the field army when it is formed. It was assumed by Congress that the deputy chief

3. Information concerning the War Department and the army was obtained mainly from *Senate Document,* No. 91, 76th Congress, 1st Session. It was submitted to the Senate by Mr. Sheppard of Texas and is published by the Government Printing Office. Information on subsequent changes has been obtained from the press and from official statements by responsible authorities of the War Department.

would succeed as chief, an arrangement that would prevent any interruption in the War Department's activities. The act was not intended to restrict the powers of the President, who, as Commander in Chief of the Army and Navy, can relieve any officer from command at any time. In case of war the President may retain the Chief of Staff in Washington if he desires and appoint another officer to command the field army.

The Chief of Staff is charged with planning, developing and executing the army's program of national defense. Aiding him are three deputy chiefs of staff, who have authority to act in the absence of the Chief of Staff, and five assistant chiefs of staff. The deputy chiefs of staff coördinate the activities of the five assistants, who head the five divisions of the War Department's General Staff. These divisions are known as G-1, G-2, G-3, G-4 and W.P.D. or War Plans Division. The Chief of the Personnel Division is known as G-1 and supervises the plans for obtaining, conserving and replacing personnel. The Chief of the Military Intelligence Division is G-2, who collects, evaluates and disseminates military information. The Chief of the Operations and Training

Division, G-3, supervises such training and operations of the military forces as are not expressly assigned to General Headquarters. G-4 is the Chief of the Supply and Maintenance Division. The Chief of the War Plans Division is responsible for the plans for employing the armed forces. The General Staff of the War Department is an operating agency which must not invade the domain of other agencies in the department if it is to obtain the best results. G-1 coöperates with the chiefs of arms and with the Adjutant General's Department in matters of personnel; G-3 coöperates with all chiefs of arms in the training programs, and G-4 with the Quartermaster, Engineer, and Medical Corps. G-2 provides information, and the War Plans Division supplies plans for the entire army.

The Infantry is the principal combat arm. Its weapons are pistols, rifles, hand grenades, automatic rifles, machine guns, antitank guns, and small mortars. It proceeds to the battlefield and fights on foot and in tanks. The Infantry forms the main fighting part of an army just as battleships form the main battle line of a fleet. The Cavalry is the fast-moving, fighting and reconnaissance arm; it fights on horseback, in armored cars, or in combat cars that are much like tanks. Comparable to the scouting forces of the navy, it precedes the main army and explores the ground ahead of the Infantry. Coöperating with observation planes of the Air Corps, it seeks to locate the enemy's main force, to drive back the enemy Cavalry and thus to protect its own forces from surprise attack. The Cavalry employs lighter weapons than those used by the Infantry, and they include pistols, rifles, machine guns and mortars.

The Field Artillery supports the Infantry and the Cavalry with its light, medium and heavy artillery. Its weapons are of many calibers, from the famous "75" firing a 15-pound shell to an 8-inch howitzer firing a 200-pound shell. Its guns have ranges from 9,000 to 19,-000 yards. A fast-moving arm, the Field Artillery can operate with the Cavalry.

The Coast Artillery operates with the field army and with the fleet. Its function is to protect the important cities and harbors of the United States and important strategic centers such as the Panama Canal, the Hawaiian Islands and Manila. Its weapons include rapid-fire guns, guns of 3 to 6 inches to protect mine fields from sweeping operations, guns of medium caliber—6, 8 or 10 inches—for use against small ships; and guns of 12, 14 and 16 inches to beat off attacks of battleships. Guns mounted on shore have a great advantage over guns mounted on ships and only very special circumstances would justify ships exposing themselves to their accurate fire.

The Air Corps attacks the enemy air forces and ground troops and bombs supply depots, factories and military installations. Three basic types of combat planes are used: pursuit, bombing, and observation. Pursuit planes include two types, the interceptor and the fighter. Interceptors meet and attack hostile aircraft approaching American territory or threatening American forces; fighter planes accompany bombardment planes to protect them from enemy pursuit planes. The bombardment planes are divided into three types, light, medium and heavy. Light bombardment furnish fire support to ground troops by machine-gun fire and bombs. Medium bombardment carry out bombardment or reconnaissance tasks that do not require extreme range. Heavy bombardment perform long-range missions and reconnaissance flights over land or sea. Observation planes furnish short-range observation, photographic, command, courier and liaison service to corps and divisions. Observation service includes visual and photographic reconnaissance and air-to-ground radio communication. All combat planes are armed with machine guns for self-defense against hostile planes and are designed for as much speed and maneuverability as their weight and engines and design permit. Planes vary in the amount of armor they have, and are to be provided with puncture-proof gasoline tanks.

Aircraft, like surface ships of the navy, are constantly undergoing changes in design, as each designer seeks to develop the maximum in speed and in offensive and defensive power. All these qualities cannot be embodied in one type. Planes vary according to their function; already bombers resemble battleships with their hitting power, observation planes suggest cruisers, and the fighting planes that escort bombers suggest the destroyers that seek to protect battleships from submarine attack. Although primarily organized to operate with the army over the land, the Air Corps can also operate with the navy against enemy ships or planes.

The Engineer Corps builds and maintains roads, bridges and shelter for the combat arms, conducts military mining, and in case of stabilized war or siege operations would construct saps, countermines, and repair enemy damage to fortifications. The combat regiments of the engineers are in the advanced sector of the combat zone. The Signal Corps maintains the communications for divisions and larger units except in the advance battle areas where the Infantry, Cavalry and Field Artillery are responsible for their own communications. The Signal Corps also operates the army radio system which connects the War Department with Corps Area Headquarters at home and Department Headquarters overseas. Although its telephones and radios are modernized, the corps still trains carrier pigeons for emergency communications with the frontline troops, to be used when all other means of communication have been destroyed by the enemy. Like the Engineer the Signal Corps is fully exposed to enemy attacks in the combat zone.

The Armored Force, the latest addition to

the fighting arms, corresponds roughly to the German Panzer divisions; on April 1, 1941, it included the First, Second, Third and Fourth Armored Divisions. The training of the First and Second Armored Divisions had advanced sufficiently to justify assembling them into a corps, the First Armored Corps of the United States Army. The Third Armored Division forming at Camp Polk, Louisiana, and the Fourth at Pine Camp, New York, will probably become the Second Armored Corps when their divisional training is complete. Present head-quarters for the Armored Force is Fort Knox, Kentucky; indications are that the force will eventually be established as a separate arm, comparable to the Infantry or Artillery, with a Chief of Branch in Washington.

The services of the War Department assist the fighting arms by relieving them of supply and administrative duties, and the care of the sick and wounded. The Adjutant General's Department records, authenticates and issues the orders of the Secretary of War and the Chief of Staff; it is responsible for enrolling reserve officers and military cadets, and re-cruiting the enlisted personnel; it supervises the administration of the War Department, and has officer representatives on the staffs of commanders of larger units and territorial areas to supervise administration. As a quasi-personnel bureau it resembles the Bureau of Navigation in the Navy Department, and co-operates with G-1, the personnel branch of the General Staff. The Inspector General's Department inspects the various commands at unexpected times, reports the conditions found and makes recommendations for improvements; it is also prepared to investigate any suspected irregularities at the order of the department. The function of the Judge Advocate General's Department is to take any legal measures found necessary by the inspector general and to advise the Secretary of War on all legal questions. The Quartermaster Corps obtains and furnishes food, clothing, equipment and shelter; the Finance Department pays out and accounts for the funds appropriated for the army.

The Ordnance Department designs, obtains and distributes to the arms and services their weapons and ammunition. It also stores and preserves ammunition and weapons in peacetime. There are six manufacturing arsenals: at Watertown, Massachusetts; Dover, New Jer-

sey; Philadelphia, Pennsylvania; Rock Island,
Illinois; Springfield, Massachusetts; and Wa-
tervliet, New York—these have been expanded,
and others are under construction. The largest proving ground at present is at Aberdeen,
Maryland.

The Chemical Warfare Service is organized
to defend the army against all types of chemical agents, including lethal gas, and is prepared to retaliate promptly if these weapons
are used. Its research and development center
is at Edgewood Arsenal in Maryland. It has
small detachments of troops at army posts to
assist in training components of the army. It
also assists the navy and trains navy personnel
in its preparations against chemical warfare.

To care for the sick and wounded the Medical Department sends its regiments with the
army into the combat zone, where stretcher-
bearers and advance dressing stations accompany the front-line troops into battle. Its personnel should be regarded as genuine combat
troops.

All branches and services of the army have
the same basic organization. The smallest unit
or squad has a war strength of 12 men or less,
and is commanded by a sergeant or corporal.

Above that comes the section of 20 or 25 men under the command of a sergeant. The next unit is the platoon of 40 or 45 men commanded by a first or second lieutenant; in the Air Corps it is called the "subflight." The company is the next unit, composed of 80 to 200 men under the command of a captain. It corresponds to the "battery" of the Field or Coast Artillery, the "troop" in the Cavalry, and the "flight" in the Air Corps. The battalion of 300 to 850 men is commanded by a major or lieutenant colonel. Its corresponding member in the Cavalry and in the Air Corps is known as the "squadron." The regiment has 800 to 3,100 men and is commanded by a colonel. It corresponds to the "group" in the Air Corps. Practically all the arms and services are organized into units ranging from the squad to the regiment. The unit known as the brigade, composed of 5,000 to 6,300 men under a brigadier general, is to be found in the Infantry, Cavalry, Field Artillery, and Coast Artillery. Corresponding units in the Air Corps are called "wings."

Only the Infantry and (more rarely) the Cavalry are formed into divisions, which are commanded by major generals. There are two types of Infantry division, the triangular (streamlined) and the square. The triangular division contains 3 Infantry regiments, 2 regiments of Field Artillery, 1 battalion each of Engineer, Medical and Quartermaster troops, and a company of Signal Corps troops with a total strength of 12,500, about 7,200 of which is Infantry. The square division contains 2 Infantry brigades, each of 2 regiments (4 regiments of Infantry), a brigade of 3 regiments of Field Artillery, 1 regiment each of Engineer, Quartermaster and Medical troops, and smaller units of Ordnance and Signal Corps specialists to make a total strength of about 18,500, of which about 10,600 is Infantry. Cavalry, Air Corps and Chemical Warfare units and additional tanks, Field Artillery and Engineers are often temporarily added to support an Infantry division.

Equipped for rapid movement, the Cavalry has no men on foot. The division or the brigade is unusual; the unit most often employed is the regiment, which consists of 8 troops—headquarters, service, reconnaissance, machine-gun, and 4 combat-car troops. The heaviest weapon of the Cavalry is the 4.2-inch mortar; its striking power is in the 4 combat troops using cars resembling tanks and armed with machine guns. Two mechanized Cavalry regiments would form a brigade, which would have the support of mechanized Field Artillery units and combat aviation.

Two or more divisions, plus whatever other troops were necessary, such as labor battalions or aviators, form a corps and would be commanded by a major general or lieutenant general. Two or more corps, plus certain units from several arms and services, form an army, commanded by a lieutenant general or general. The United States has four armies.

All other units assigned by the War Department to the field forces are included in the general term G.H.Q. troops, that is, troops at the disposal of the Commander in Chief in the Field, and which he can attach or assign, temporarily or permanently as needed, to the various field armies. Troops not so assigned are retained under the War Department control in the zones of the interior, which may comprise the whole of the United States. The dispositions made by Joffre in February 1916 before the battle of Verdun will illustrate the methods of G.H.Q.; 50 French divisions under the Commanders of the Groups of Armies (comparable to the 4 American Army Commanders) held the front line, with 20 divisions at their disposition in reserve, while Joffre retained 25 divisions under his own direction at G.H.Q. which he employed initially to stem the German attack.

As already stated, the elementary military training of the army is supervised by the chiefs of arms; that is, the chiefs of Infantry, Field Artillery, and Air Corps. Some of these chiefs are also responsible for the procurement of material as well as for the basic training of their personnel. Each of the old established branches has its own training center, which is usually under the direct supervision of the chief of the branch. The Cavalry center is at Fort Riley, Kansas; that for the Artillery at Fort Sill, Oklahoma; that for the Infantry at Fort Benning, Georgia; both at Fort Benning and at Fort Knox, Kentucky, elementary instruction is given to the newly organized Armored Force. The Air Corps has direct supervision of several training centers, in California, Texas and other states. But since it is responsible for training its personnel in combination with other arms, it has to be in all echelons of the General Staff. Only in this way would there be any assurance of a thorough consideration of the powers and limitations of the airplane. In coöperation with the Infantry the Air Corps has recently undertaken the training of parachutists, a development that shows how seriously are taken the lessons of the current war in Europe. With the present program of expansion (1941), every branch of the army has been forced to enlarge its existing facilities and to establish others. The Armored Force may find, as it gains more experience in its special task, that it will require its own training area with wider spaces to meet the demands of extreme mobility.

The Chief of the General Staff, the Corps Commanders, the Army Commanders, and finally the Commanding General of the Field Army supervise the training and organization of the combined arms, Infantry, Cavalry, Artillery, the Armored Forces, the Air Forces, into similar homogeneous units of regiments, brigades, divisions, army corps, armies and finally into the American Field Army. To accomplish this object the army has divided the United States into nine corps areas, with a commanding general in each area; overseas we have departments: the Philippine, Hawaiian,

Panama Canal, and Puerto Rican. The corps areas bordering the coasts and the Great Lakes coincide with one or more naval districts having an admiral as commandant; overseas wherever there is an army department there is a naval district or station with an admiral or captain as commandant. Coöperation between them is obtained as in Washington by means of joint boards which provide cross-connections between all units of the army and navy. The 9 corps areas perform all overhead duties; the field forces concentrate on training. There are 33 active divisions, 26 infantry, 1 motorized, 4 armored, 2 horse cavalry, grouped in 9 army corps and 2 armored corps. The armored corps are assigned to G.H.Q. The I, II, and VI army corps form the First Army, headquarters New York; VII army corps and 2d Cavalry division, the Second Army, headquarters Memphis; IV, V, VIII army corps, 1st Cavalry division and 56th Cavalry brigade, the Third Army, headquarters San Antonio; III, IX army corps, Fourth Army, headquarters San Francisco. Areas can be altered and their headquarters changed. Each corps area is capable of recruiting and maintaining at least one army corps; after the corps is formed it has its own commander, a major general or lieutenant general, not to be confused with the commander of the corps area from which the corps came.

When the Chief of Staff becomes Commanding General of the Field Army, he will need at his General Headquarters (usually written G.H.Q.) a general staff, including a chief of staff, a deputy chief of staff and five assistants, G-1, G-2, G-3, G-4 and War Plans Division, an administrative and service staff, an adjutant general, a chief quartermaster, a chief surgeon, an inspector general, and his personal aides—altogether a very numerous staff. In peacetime a nucleus of this G.H.Q. staff is maintained with a major general at the head who is prepared to become chief of staff to the Commanding General. To complete this staff, some officers from the War Department General Staff will be added, thus insuring that those who will be charged with the execution of the department's war plan will be familiar with its development and the preparation of the army to execute it. The peacetime staff is sufficiently large to permit the Commanding General to establish General Headquarters in the field immediately on mobilization or earlier if desired.

When the Commanding General takes over G.H.Q., he commands all armies assigned to G.H.Q. by the War Department. Whenever he is operating in the United States, he controls the distribution and operation of all troops assigned to his command in the interior of the United States or on any of the frontiers. A new Chief of Staff of the Army would continue to operate from Washington as Chief of Staff for the Secretary of War; he would probably be the former deputy chief of staff. If desirable for administrative purposes, the Secretary of War could rearrange the corps areas and the zone of the interior, which would continue under the jurisdiction of the War Department. If the army should be sent overseas it would probably be called the American Expeditionary Force; all the continental United States would then be designated a zone of the interior and administered through corps area commanders by the War Department.

Although the peacetime Chief of Staff is the logical choice to command the field army, all senior officers of the army are familiar with the provisions for establishing a field army and the requirements to make it effective. Any Commanding General selected by the President would report for this command with a definite idea of his duties and the immediate measures necessary to expand the peacetime organization to meet the conditions of war.

In addition to the G.H.Q. staff a general staff is furnished each division commander, each corps commander, each Army Commander, each Commander of a Group of Armies. These staffs are organized alike, each with a deputy chief of staff, a G-1, G-2, G-3, G-4, and a W.P.D., each deputy and assistant chief in every echelon having corresponding duties. They are literally the general's staff, and officers have been trained for their duties with the same care that regimental officers are trained for infantry or artillery duty. General staff officers are often criticized by military experts who frequently know a better way to win a war, but they have been selected from their colleagues for their mental capacity and are usually the hardest-worked and -working officers in an army. They are members of a team and the credit or discredit for what they do goes to the commander. But in officer messes where campaigns are discussed in detail and in lectures at officers' schools, proper staff officers get a generous measure of praise from brother officers who know the value of good staff work from their own war experience.

The Chief of Staff and the assistant chiefs of staff act as lobes of the brain of the Secretary of War and of their Commanding General, and in the department or in the field a proper staff functions as harmoniously as the intellect of one great man. In the campaign of the Marne, Joffre kept control of the entire French Army throughout the retreat from the frontiers to the gates of Paris by means of the staff, which he dispatched from place to place, wherever the situation was critical, to explain his intentions to his widely separated subordinate commanders. In Joffre's opinion members of his staff were the "exponents of the very brain and will of the commander in chief," and by his skilful employment of highly trained assistants and his own firm resolve he showed at the Marne that "in spite of all difficulties, a battle could and should be directed."

The War Department may be overorganized, and undoubtedly some offices overlap, but the organization is comprehensive and sound. If a Secretary of War selects a proper Chief of Staff and competent chiefs of arms and bureaus, he has an organization well adapted to create and operate armies in the field. Unfortunately the War Department has not had a field army to operate since 1919, and only by actual experience can officers prepare themselves to command large units. The army lacks general officers who have demonstrated their capacity to handle large forces in the field in peacetime.

In spite of the efforts of President Theodore Roosevelt, the Navy Department was not provided with a General Staff. During the last World War the Office of Naval Operations was established, but Congress withheld from the Chief of Naval Operations the control of chiefs of bureaus possessed by the Chief of Staff of the Army. The Office of Naval Operations greatly improved the organization of the Navy Department and offers a Secretary who wishes to use it and who will supplement the authority conferred by Congress on the Chief of Naval Operations an effective instrument to coordinate and control the activities of the department in Washington, the naval shore establishments and the forces afloat.

Some subdivisions of Naval Operations are almost identical with some of the General Staff of the War Department: the Division of Naval Intelligence and the Navy War Plans Division correspond with G-2 and War Plans Division of the War Department. A Fleet Training Division and a Ships Movement Division in Naval Operations perform many of the duties of G-3, the Operations and Training Division of the General Staff. The duties of G-1 are paralleled in the Bureau of Navigation, which supervises the elementary training of officers and men, while the Chief of Naval Operations and the Commanders in Chief of the Pacific, Atlantic and Asiatic Fleets are responsible for the training of fleet units and the fleets. There is a Material Division in Operations that resembles in some respects G-4, the Supply and Maintenance Division of the General Staff. The activities of Naval Operations are coördinated by the assistant chief of operations who is comparable to the deputy chief of staff. General Staff officers of the army, after being trained at the Command and General Staff College and the Army War College, are regularly detailed to the General Staff for four years, when they are returned to duty with troops. Officers selected for staff duty in the fleet or in Naval Operations are usually, but not necessarily, graduates of the Naval War College. The staffs of various naval units are not identical and practically interchangeable as they are in the army, but they are approximately alike, and a staff officer from one fleet unit would have no difficulty in coöperating with his corresponding officer on the staff of another unit commander. The staffs of the Commanders of the Battle Force and the Scouting Force, the two major subdivisions of the United States Pacific Fleet, are practically identical and include (1) a chief of staff; (2) operations officer; (3) force engineer officer; (4) force gunnery officer; (5) flag secretary; (6) flag lieutenant; (7) communication officer; (8) aerological officer; (9) force surgeon; (10) force paymaster and (11) force constructor.

The chief of staff is the executive officer of the commander of the force; he can act in the name of his commander. The operations officer is assistant to the chief of staff and is responsible for operations and tactical training of the force. The gunnery officer supervises the gunnery training, assists the operations officer and the chief of staff, and coördinates the gunnery officers of individual ships and other units of the force. The force engineer inspects the engineering plants of the various ships, gives technical advice when needed and supervises the engineering activities of the force. His primary responsibility is to make sure that the engineering plants of the ships are in condition to carry them to the battlefield, ready in every respect for a fight. Theodore Roosevelt continually reminded the fleet that the only shots that count are those that hit the target. One well-known admiral added the admonition that the finest gunnery ship in the fleet was of no use if her engines could not carry her to the scene of action. The engineer officer coöperates closely with the force constructor who has similar responsibilities for the ships' hulls and fittings, except the armament, which comes under the gunnery officer. The flag secretary is responsible for official correspondence and the dissemination of information and orders sent by mail; the flag lieutenant for all visual signals; and the communication officer for all radio communications. Obviously these officers must work closely together for these three means of communication supplement each other. The aerological officer is selected from a small group of officers who have been trained to observe and predict the weather, especially probable flying conditions. The communication officer, the engineer officer and the gunnery officer are usually selected from officers who have specialized in their subjects. The force surgeon advises the commander in all matters affecting the health of the personnel and inspects the surgical departments of the ships; the force paymaster is responsible for fleet supplies and must be ready to pay the crews twice a month.

The staffs of the Battle and Scouting Forces assist the commanders in the operations and maintenance of both forces. The Commander in Chief of the Pacific Fleet entrusts the maintenance of the two forces to their immediate commanders, which gives him more time to consider the operations and tactics of the fleet. His staff is primarily organized for operations and battle and does not usually include a force constructor, surgeon and paymaster; but the operations officer, whose task is greater, is given one or more assistants.

The staffs of smaller units of the fleet do not include as many officers, but they have to do all staff work in connection with operations. Among the lower echelons, such as a destroyer flotilla, there would be an operations officer, a flag secretary, an engineer officer, gunnery officer, radio officer and flag lieutenant.

Naval officers usually are good administrators; they have worked together ashore and afloat, are genuinely interested in the efficiency of the navy, and by voluntary coöperation ordinarily compensate for the defective organization of the department and the lack of training for staff duties as compared with the army. But a government department should not be dependent upon voluntary coöperation; the Chief of Naval Operations should be given legal authority over the bureaus.

The United States Fleets are properly organized under the Commanders in Chief, although the staffs of the various commanders are not uniform or interchangeable and may be unnecessarily large. Naval officers complain that the paper work in the fleets is excessive. The fleets are active, efficient organizations well prepared to operate in any part of the world except in the Arctic regions. The United States Fleets are living, growing institutions; they have their own personality, which is stamped on the personnel from whom loyalty and devoted service are demanded and usually obtained. Naval officers generally are convinced that the Navy Department and shore establishments exist only to serve the fleets; and as far as their authority extends, insist that appropriations be spent on projects that increase the strength of the fleets.

American navy yards are under the military control of line officers but are provided with an industrial manager, either a naval constructor or engineer, who is in direct charge of the construction and repair facilities. The line-officer commandant is responsible for the yards being operated for the benefit of the fleets. Most of our navy yards are on the east coast, at Portsmouth, Boston, New York, Philadelphia, Hampton Roads, Charleston, Key West, Pensacola, and New Orleans. On the west coast there are yards at Bremerton on Puget Sound, and at San Francisco, and a small one at San Diego. There are yards of varying sizes at Olongapo and Cavite in the Manila area; in the Canal Zone; at Guantanamo in Cuba; and at San Juan, Puerto Rico.

The industrial experience gained in the yards and bureaus by naval officers facilitates their intercourse with businessmen; in general they are more familiar than army officers with industrial practices and business customs. Secretary Meyer concentrated practically all navy purchases, which are large, under the Bureau of Supplies and Accounts; as a result bureaus never bid against each other; one bureau is never oversupplied while another lacks an essential raw material. Similarly naval constructors and engineer officers are familiar with private construction and ship design, as well as the business customs of private shipbuilders. In this respect the Navy Department is better organized than the War Department—when it obtains appropriations it can quickly make its contracts, for the Bureau of Ships and the Bureau of Ordnance know the facilities of the shipyards and factories capable of meeting navy requirements.

Naval aviation, an integral part of the United States Navy, is trained to operate with the fleets at sea. The Naval Bureau of Aeronautics is primarily responsible for procurement of material and personnel, and for the training of the personnel until they are absorbed into the fleets when the Commanders in Chief become responsible for their fleet training. The principal training stations for naval aviators are at Pensacola, Florida, and San Diego, California.

With the fleets are aircraft carriers, whose planes are catapulted or take off and return to the flight deck; battleships and cruisers, which can only catapult their planes; and patrol planes or flying boats that take off or land in the water. Among them is every type of plane, fighting, observation, small bomber, large bomber and torpedo plane, including amphibians.

Navy flying boats accompany the fleets in almost all weathers, sailing over and around them; they can carry heavy loads of bombs, and are trained to act with the fleets on the offensive or defensive. They are supplied by mother ships similar to those used for submarines and destroyers. These patrol squadrons have flown in formation to Honolulu, Alaska, Panama, and the Philippine Islands so often that such flights are considered routine. The General Headquarters Air Force of the Army is analogous to naval patrol squadrons in its operations. Both can support the United States Fleets on either the offensive or defensive. In a campaign near our own overseas bases the fleets could be reënforced by army and navy planes with a smaller cruising radius.

Strategy used to be two-dimensional, on

land and sea; now it embraces land, sea and air. And the next naval battle will be three-dimensional—on the surface, under the surface and in the air. War on the sea is not a question of surface ships versus air ships or subsurface craft; only on rare occasions and in isolated encounters will surface ships be pitted against aircraft or submarines. In general hostile aircraft will have to defeat the navy fighting planes before they can attack surface vessels of the United States Fleets or any of their subdivisions; and submarines will have to penetrate a destroyer screen to launch a torpedo against a capital ship. And in a typical naval engagement the commander will be required to coordinate these different arms.

Operating at sea, the fleets have always been dependent upon the army to hold the continental and overseas bases; today the army can contribute its bombing squadrons, and in some instances fighting and scouting planes to participate directly with the fleets before, during and after battle. More than ever before coöperation between the army and navy is essential.

Substantial accord between the Chief of Naval Operations and the Chief of the General Staff on joint professional problems affecting

both services is necessary to assure cordial cooperation between the army and navy; a similar harmony of opinion is necessary between
the Chief of Naval Operations and the Commanders in Chief of the United States Fleets,
and between the Chief of Staff of the War Department in Washington and the Commanding General of the Field Army, if each service
is to operate at maximum efficiency. The friction and burden of war put severe strains on
the tempers and personalities of the military
and naval leaders. A President and the Secretaries of War and Navy should assure themselves of the mutual goodwill and agreement
on technical questions among their professional advisers in time of peace, or discord between the two services is certain to arise.

During war a President of the United States
could not divest himself of his responsibilities
as Commander in Chief of the Army and Navy
if he desired; in the execution of these important duties he is usually an amateur and will
have to depend upon the advice of his professional chiefs of the army and navy. This handi-
cap is not peculiar to democratic governments.
In spite of his many uniforms Emperor William II was an amateur; today the rulers of

the Axis powers are amateurs. Democracies can be as well served as autocracies, and among the officers of the two services a President can find chiefs who have already proved their competence in their peacetime duties. These same officers may fail under the additional strain of war; Lincoln was compelled to change several of his generals, and if the Confederate Navy had been relatively as strong as its army he would have been compelled to relieve some flag officers of the navy.

Army and naval officers like all other professional men sometimes differ in their views. A President should accept the advice only of the officer who will have to take the responsibility if failure ensues; advice from any other comes without that sobering influence. If a President loses confidence in his legal military and naval advisers he should replace them. Lloyd George continued Field Marshals Robertson and Haig in their positions when he no longer trusted them, with resulting dissension among the High Command that contributed to the British defeat of March 1918.

Civil heads of the state who approve recommendations of their military chiefs should share the responsibility of failure and shield their military leaders from an uninformed public indignation, provided the plans of the campaign have been competently and vigorously executed. In war many doubtful enterprises must be undertaken; success can never be guaranteed. The first Pitt inspired his generals and admirals to their utmost endeavors because they were convinced he would support them even if defeated, provided they had exerted themselves to the utmost. Lincoln bravely shared the criticism heaped on Grant after the bloody repulse at Cold Harbor, although he knew Grant had erred. Clemenceau defended Foch in the Chamber of Deputies although his failure to anticipate the direction of the German offensive exposed Paris to capture. Confidence that he will be supported by the head of his government will nerve the heart and strengthen the judgment of a Commander in Chief at sea or ashore, in those hours of perplexity when wisdom and courage are taxed to the utmost, and will enable him to determine and pursue to the end a correct military decision, regardless of enemy opposition.

CHAPTER FOUR

THE POSITION OF THE UNITED STATES IN THE FAR EAST

THE discussion of the American position in the Far East usually includes the question of the independence or the retention of the Philippine Islands and the tactical problems involved in their defense. The problem of the Philippines is only a part of American policy in the Far East, and that in turn is only a part of our general foreign policy; similarly the defense of the Philippines is only a part of the larger problem of national defense. The natural approach to the Far Eastern policy and the defense of the Philippines is to consider them in relation to American foreign policy and national defense as a whole.

The two cornerstones of American foreign policy are the Monroe Doctrine and the open door in China. In the twentieth century Great Britain, like the United States a satisfied nation, has acquiesced in these two principles, which, when effective, insure equal opportunities for all nations to trade with Spanish America and the Far East, while maintaining the territorial integrity of these areas against the expansionist tendencies of growing states in Europe and Asia. The increasing strength of Germany in Europe, the creation of the German Fleet and the rivalry between Germany and England caused the concentration of the British Fleet in its own home waters. Thus the two large European fleets were kept within European confines. The construction of the Panama Canal, the defeat of Germany in the last World War, and the continued acceptance of the Monroe Doctrine by the British Government made possible the transfer of the United States Fleet to the Pacific at a time when the general world situation had left only Russia and Japan capable of challenging the open-door policy. There ensued an unacknowledged but effective coöperation between the British and American policies and navies in support of the Monroe Doctrine and, to a lesser extent, of the open-door policy in China.

Except for the action of Russia in making a nonaggression pact with Germany in 1939, the present grouping of belligerent states, includ-

ing the openly expressed sympathy of the
United States for Great Britain and the adherence of Japan to the Axis powers, resulted
from easily understood causes. Great Britain
and France with their large empires and the
United States by its support of the Monroe
Doctrine and the open-door policy denied to
Germany, Italy and Japan the expansion
which they felt was necessary and justified.
The common desire of these three countries
for more territory furnished a basis for concerted action against the three powers which
stood in their way. Hitler has secured the be-
nevolent neutrality of Russia by permitting
her to recover territory lost in the World War,
and until now has been able to reconcile the
differences between Stalin and Mussolini, and
between Russia and Japan. The differences
between Stalin and Mussolini are largely the
result of different ideologies which have developed since the World War and may be settled more easily than the longer-lived Russo-
Japanese antagonism that has existed since the
1870's. The war in China has lessened Japan's
value as an ally and her long rivalry with Russia will make it difficult for them to coöperate.
The military weakness of Italy renders her

amenable to Hitler's suggestions, but has thrown an additional strain on Germany, while the collapse of France has rendered the position of Great Britain in the Atlantic critical. The American Government with popular and congressional approval has promised all aid short of war to Great Britain, China and Greece.

The impact of these events on American foreign policy has created a new strategic problem for the United States, namely, to safeguard its interests in the western Pacific and to be prepared to defend its continental area and the Western Hemisphere, if the Axis powers gain control of the Atlantic. Because Japan's open alignment with Germany has convinced Americans that she must be considered a potential enemy, public opinion has supported Congress in increasing the navy and supplying the personnel to man the fleet. The greatest danger from Japan, a surprise attack on the unguarded Pacific Fleet, lying at anchor in San Pedro Harbor, under peacetime conditions, has already been averted. The Pacific Fleet is at one of the strongest bases in the world—Pearl Harbor—practically on a war footing and under a war regime. There will be no American Port Arthur.

The Japanese Government has stated that the commercial facilities in the Marshall, Caroline and Mariana groups have been improved, which would make some of them available as air and submarine bases. It has never approved requests of American men-of-war to visit these islands to ascertain if they had been fortified. Such fortification would be contrary to the terms of the mandate. In a campaign in the western Pacific the American Commander in Chief must assume that several of these islets have facilities for small craft and planes and may be fortified as well. These tiny islands lie well away from the direct route to Manila except in the neighborhood of Guam.

Some naval students have asserted that Japanese possession of these islands would block the advance of the American Fleet from Honolulu to Manila. A study of the chart of the Pacific, and of the results of the air and naval engagements in the Mediterranean during the present war, will lead to a contrary opinion. These islands are diminutive, their tortuous channels are formed by coral reefs which open into small atolls that are made to serve as harbors. Their sand-covered shores rarely rise higher than ten feet and will grow only stunted palmettos, except for a few of the larger ones which have some coconut groves and export a small amount of copra. Drinking water is scarce and brackish, and while fish, coconuts and on some of them breadfruit, can be obtained, all other supplies must be imported.

In the Mediterranean, Italian air and submarine bases in southern Italy, Sicily, Sardinia, Pantelleria and the Dodecanese Islands are much nearer the routes of the British convoys that have passed between Alexandria and Gibraltar than any of these less developed bases in the mandated islands are to the route between Honolulu and Manila. The Marshall and Caroline Islands contain small harbors in Jaluit, Kusaie, Truk, Ponape, Wotje and Eniwetok that could shelter submarines and aircraft. Eniwetok is 400 miles from the direct route to Manila, the other harbors are more distant. In the neighborhood of Guam the fleet must pass within 30 miles of Rota and 100 miles of Saipan, both of which have air fields, while Saipan can also shelter submarines. Beyond Guam, the island of Yap, important because of its cable stations, has a harbor that could shelter planes and submarines. It is over 250 miles from the route to San Bernardino Strait; Malakal Harbor in the Pelew Islands is in the same vicinity but more distant from the Strait. If the American Fleet passes north of Luzon it will approach the southern extremity of Formosa and the Pescadores Islands, which have the nearest naval base to Luzon that has been regularly developed by Japan. The Pescadores can shelter the entire Japanese Fleet, and it is in that area and not along the route to the San Bernardino Strait that the Japanese Fleet will become a threat to the American ships.

The elements of strategy show that the flank of an advancing fleet is a poor place to station submarines and aircraft; it is too much to hope that the Japanese Commander in Chief will make such a faulty disposition of his numerically inferior fleet.

The submarine and the airplane have added to the problems confronting the American commander but they have presented even more perplexities to the Japanese commander; war is always a choice of difficulties and the Japanese have the harder choice. Japan's ally,

Germany, has already threatened to sink every American merchantman approaching the British Isles; if Japan follows Germany's example American submarines can sink every Japanese ship they encounter approaching the Japanese islands. If the Japanese bomb Manila, Tokio is equally vulnerable. American submarines can keep a periscope watch off the exits of the Inland Sea or the Pescadores Islands, and can follow the Japanese Fleet to sea. In short, there is no method of approach or attack open to the Japanese Navy and Air Force to which the American cannot reply in equal or in greater measure.

Although Germany is very powerful in Europe, her enemies, present and potential, are more powerful in the Pacific. On the whole Japan loses by joining Germany and Italy. China would be of great assistance to the United States by absorbing Japanese forces; the naval and air forces of Holland in the East Indies would be of considerable value to the United States, and the Dutch islands could supply fuel for the fleet. The greatest aid, however, is to be expected from Great Britain and Australasia. If the well-equipped and fortified naval base at Singapore was at the service of the American Fleet, most of the difficulties of a campaign in the western Pacific would disappear.

The construction of the base at Singapore throws an interesting side light on Anglo-American relations. Japan was not the only country to profit by the last World War. While the United States was neutral American merchants in China displaced British and German who could no longer supply their customers. British merchants naturally resented their displacement, and bad feeling arose between British and American competitors, which did not disappear after the United States entered the war. British naval officers resented the rapid growth of the American Navy during the war, and when the British Prime Minister Lloyd George and his First Lord of the Admiralty suggested to Secretary of the Navy Daniels and Admiral Benson in 1919 that it revert to its former relative inferiority to the British Navy, the resentment in the American Navy at least equaled British irritation. The postwar differences between Great Britain and the United States were nowhere more evident than in the Far East and among officers of the two navies. President Wilson indignantly rejected Lloyd George's proposal. When President Harding called the Naval Limitations Conference many American naval officers, convinced that it had been inspired in London because the British taxpayers were unable to support a naval building program, were as suspicious of British as of Japanese proposals. Their suspicions were increased when the cool-headed Admiral Baron Kato made the demilitarization of Hong Kong, Manila and Guam the price of Japanese agreement to limitation, and the astute Mr. Balfour amended the limits to permit the creation of an empire base at Singapore. The American delegation, intent on securing an agreement, made no effort to except Guam or Manila from the military restrictions.

Balfour won the real victory, for Singapore, commanding one of the most important waterways of the world, where the Indian and Pacific oceans meet, is more valuable than either Hong Kong or Shanghai to Imperial defense. Singapore secures the northeastern exits of the Indian Ocean; Australia dominates the southeastern shores; India, Burma and other British possessions control its northern arms, the Bay of Bengal and the Arabian Sea; from Aden to

Cape Town British possessions in East and South Africa control its western shores and the passage to the Atlantic. In the whole basin of the Indian Ocean only Japan could threaten British security. Ramsay MacDonald's two governments almost prevented and did delay the construction of the defenses and facilities of Singapore until February 1938, in spite of the demands of Australia, New Zealand, India, Burma, the Malay States and the Straits Settlements that the work be expedited. In October 1940 the British cabinet announced that the project as originally conceived was complete, and early in 1941 reënforcements from Australia and New Zealand landed in Singapore and proceeded at once to previously prepared positions in the Malay Peninsula to protect the fortress from an overland Japanese attack by way of Thailand.

The fortifications were constructed simultaneously with the facilities, and before the King George VI graving dock was opened the defenses were subjected to the test of a simulated Japanese attack. The British Asiatic Fleet represented the enemy, the regular garrison of about 10,000, assisted by submarines and aircraft that had flown from Iraq and India, undertook the defense. This operation indicates the proper method of defending a fortress and illustrates again that aircraft and submarines do not necessarily imperil sea power; on the contrary, used in conjunction with well-fortified bases and a preponderant fleet these two new weapons make possible its most economical exercise.

The island of Singapore is connected with the Malay Peninsula by a causeway carrying the road and the Federated Malay States railway, which furnish the only lines of communication with the mainland. The roadbeds pass through a tropical jungle and it is along the road and railway that a Japanese attack on the back door to Singapore would have to pass. In this respect the tactical situation at Singapore resembles that at Gibraltar. The permanent garrison of Singapore has been especially trained in jungle warfare with the purpose of defending the approaches to the strategic causeway: its total strength is unknown but it included British, Indian and Malay troops and with local reserves probably approximated 10,000 men. Since the war it has been reënforced until it is not less than 50,000. All except the latest arrivals have exercised at the stations they would occupy in case of attack.

The man power of the native Malays has been fully utilized in the army, navy and air force. There is one native combat regiment, and natives are enlisted in all the auxiliary services, thus relieving the British troops for the combat branches. Malays are excellent seamen and furnish the enlisted men for the mine layers and sweepers; they also perform many of the functions of ground troops for the Royal Air Force, while a regiment of Eurasians has been trained for antiaircraft batteries.

The naval base proper covers approximately four square miles. It is fully equipped to repair, refit and refuel ships; its docks are supplied with the necessary cranes to remove the heaviest guns which its shops are fitted to reline or renew; its fuel tanks are underground, and it is protected by antiaircraft batteries. Adjoining the base in the Straits of Johore is an anchorage for the heaviest ships, which will accommodate the largest fleet in the world. Singapore could repair all the ships of the Mediterranean Fleet if it became desirable to use its resources. Designed primarily as a naval base, it bids fair to become even more important as an air base. In addition to several military fields with airdromes and repair facilities, the commercial airport on the island is the best one east of Suez. There are numerous air fields in Malaya, and the Royal Air Force based on Singapore would be strategically disposed to support Hong Kong, Borneo, Port Darwin or Ceylon. Manila is the only other port in the Far East that is strategically comparable to Singapore; together they dominate the waters connecting the Indian and Pacific oceans. The details of the batteries are military secrets, but they were constructed to hold Singapore against a superior fleet and to resist an overland attack long enough to permit the arrival of reënforcements. Singapore is probably provided with 16-inch or larger guns to keep hostile battleships at a distance, 8- or 12-inch to dispose of reconnoitering cruisers, quick-firing 6-inch for enemy destroyers, 3-inch batteries for hostile mine sweepers, and machine guns to protect the water front from a surprise landing. In addition, air fields, the navy yard and important supply houses would be protected by antiaircraft batteries. Interspersed with the guns will be fixed and mobile howitzers whose high trajectory will enable them to drop heavy projectiles upon the decks of attacking ships. It is known that reserve supplies of food, particularly of rice, have been provided and a system of issue adopted that will prevent deterioration. On account of the polyglot population Singapore requires and has assumed strict control over all aliens in time of peace. Since the war the police have been reënforced with a Local Defense Corps similar to the Home Guard in the United Kingdom.

At present the approaches to Singapore are guarded by British troops, the garrison is fully manned, and mine fields are in place. The Japanese Fleet would not venture a frontal attack. The Japanese must come by way of Thailand, through the jungle, and assault the fortress from the rear or attempt a siege. Supplies and munitions could be dispatched from India or Burma, and a navy that regularly supplied Gibraltar would know how to relieve Singapore. The Japanese showed skill, courage and determination in the siege of Port Arthur; they would need all those qualities in an even more marked degree to capture Singapore. The British would not be content with a passive defense; their planes and submarines would attack the attackers; fast torpedo boats would be alert for targets, mobile howitzers would lob their heavy shells into the forward lines of the besiegers, and the defending infantry would sally forth to counterattack the approaching enemy. The British Army has shown its capacity for defense from Gibraltar to Ladysmith, and the navy has shown its skill in bringing reënforcements to its brothers in arms under the very guns of besieging armies and fleets.

Today the United States has a fleet available for use in the Far East but has an inadequate base; Great Britain has the base but her fleet is needed nearer home. If Singapore is placed at the disposal of the American Commander in Chief, his fleet can operate with vigor in the western Pacific supported by a completely equipped and heavily fortified base to refit, refuel and repair his ships. In that case Singapore would be relieved of any danger of being besieged; the advance of Japan to the southward would be halted; Indo-China, the Netherlands East Indies and Australasia would be protected. The balance in the Far East would be restored, and as the present world dislocation began there its restoration should logically start in that area.

Although the Netherlands Government has been aware of the exposed position of its East Indian empire, it has been unable to maintain a navy sufficiently strong to oppose the Japanese Fleet. But it has created a naval force of small cruisers, gunboats, destroyers, submarines, mine layers, motor torpedo boats and flying boats especially designed for operations in those waters which will give the Japanese Fleet some trouble unaided and will be a welcome increment to any fleet operating in that region. The little Netherlands Navy has distinct alliance value. In 1939 it consisted of the *Java* and the *Sumatra*, 7,000-ton cruisers carrying 10 5.9-inch guns, speed 30 knots; the *Tromp*, of 3,500 tons, carrying 6 5.9-inch guns and 6 21-inch torpedo tubes, speed 33 knots; 6 or 7 destroyers, of 1,650 tons, carrying 4 4.7-inch guns, 2 3-inch antiaircraft guns, and 6 21-inch torpedo tubes; 8 submarines of moderate size but very seaworthy craft. Each submarine is armed with 1 3.5-inch gun and the larger ones carry 8 21-inch torpedo tubes. In addition there were 40 to 50 large seaplanes, mainly Dornier flying boats, and a considerable force of observation and fighter planes. In 1939 there were also being built some 14 motor torpedo boats of 15 tons, capable of making 38 knots, and carrying 2 18-inch torpedo tubes. Since that time the Netherlanders have increased their submarines to possibly 15 and their flying boats to about 75, have added to their observation and fighter planes,[1] and have completed about a dozen of their motor torpedo boats. There are ample facilities in the islands to maintain this force and increase the number of torpedo boats.

During the past few years the moves of Japan have caused the British and Americans to co-operate in the Pacific; the friendlier feeling was openly shown when the two governments agreed to American occupation of Canton and Enderbury Islands, on the air route between Hawaii and Australasia, until their long-disputed titles could be established. The tiny islands of Baker, Howland and Jarvis were occupied first by American whalers, and became American possessions under an act of Congress

1. It is known that during the last five years Holland has been buying American-built combat planes, including observation, pursuit and torpedo planes.

which provided for their local administration.
They were wanted for their guano, but when it
was gone the islands were abandoned by the
United States. The crews of British frigates
landed and claimed them for Great Britain.
The United States never admitted the British
claim but did not contest it until Pan American Airways wished to use the islands as bases
for planes flying between the west coast and
New Zealand and Australia. This route was
given up in favor of that via Canton and Enderbury. In spite of the keen competition with
Imperial Airways, which was seeking to establish a line between Canada and New Zealand,
the two countries quickly came to an agreement which pooled the resources of the islands
and linked Canada, the United States, New
Zealand and Australia by air.

Later when Pan American shifted to a better route via Canton and Enderbury Islands in
the Phoenix group, another dispute arose over
ownership, and the result was a compromise in
1939 on the basis of joint British-American
possession for fifty years, with Pan American
allowed to construct facilities for its clippers.
The atmosphere between London and Washington was very different when this agreement

was reached from that prevailing in the early 'thirties when the navies and nations were bickering over the size and number of a few cruisers. This sentiment grew not from their greater love for each other but out of their common apprehensions of the advance of Japan in the Far East and the insistence of Australia and New Zealand on closer communications with the United States in view of the rise of Japan.

In addition to the line of air bases connecting California and New Zealand and Australia, the Hawaiian and Samoan Islands furnish direct communications between Australasia and the United States, well removed from any Japanese raiders. Pago Pago, on Tutuila Island in American Samoa, is the best harbor in the Samoan Islands. The British and American possessions in the Pacific Ocean are naturally complementary; by coöperating the two nations can control the Pacific Ocean; in addition the British would be enabled to dominate the Indian Ocean, around whose basin lies an immense part of the British Empire.

The world situation has increased the strategic importance of the Philippines for they complement the Singapore position of Great

Britain and with the Netherlands East Indies these positions could be made a natural barrier to any Japanese advance toward Australasia. But the Philippines have not become essential to national defense. In a military sense the United States is a practically invulnerable continental island fronting on the Atlantic and Pacific oceans, extending from the Canal Zone through Alaska to the Bering Sea. The United States should provide local defense for its overseas possessions in proportion to their strategic importance, to render them secure and to make them available as bases for the fleet and air forces. Overseas bases, adequately equipped and fortified, contribute to their own defense by the assistance they give the fleet in gaining and maintaining control of the sea upon which the security of all overseas possessions ultimately depends: and they justify their cost to the American taxpayers by the direct contribution they make to the defense of the continental United States by enabling naval forces operating from them to keep possible enemies at a greater distance.

American possessions overseas include the Virgin Islands, Puerto Rico, the Canal Zone, the Hawaiian Islands, Guam and the Philippines, which extend from the eastern end of the Caribbean Sea westward to the South Sea, between the equator and 22° north latitude. To these must be added the recently acquired bases in British possessions, namely, Newfoundland, Bermuda, Jamaica, the Bahamas, Antigua, St. Lucia, Trinidad and British Guiana. Improvements in aviation have increased the value of these scattered islands; properly equipped and fortified they would enable a nation possessing a superior navy and air force to dominate the greater part of the Atlantic and Pacific oceans.

Any or all of these might be useful but only Newfoundland, Bermuda, Puerto Rico, Trinidad, the Canal Zone, the Hawaiian Islands, the Galapagos and selected bases in the Aleutian Islands[2] could be considered essential to the defense of the United States. The remainder could be lost without endangering the safety of the United States; their purpose is to keep an enemy at a greater distance from the homeland and assist the fleet to protect American foreign trade and attack the enemy's. Only

2. There are under construction at present in Alaska five air bases and one submarine base. Dutch Harbor on Unalaska Island has long been used as a base for naval operations.

strategically located bases should be fortified; unnecessary bases absorb guns and men
needed elsewhere.

To visualize the military and naval position
of the United States before the addition of
British bases and with only its own responsibilities, the reader should imagine himself at
Honolulu or San Juan, Puerto Rico, rather
than at San Francisco or New York. Honolulu
is almost equally distant from Manila, 4,767
miles and San Juan, 5,678 miles, our most exposed east and west frontiers. San Juan is over
10,000 miles from Manila and 6,160 from
Punta Arenas on the Strait of Magellan, but it
is only 2,600 miles from Pernambuco where
Brazil approaches nearest to Africa, 1,600
miles from Halifax, 1,400 miles from New
York and 856 miles from Bermuda.

In case of a Japanese-American war the
United States Navy would require only the
Manila Bay area as a naval base; it would not
be necessary for military or naval purposes to
hold the entire Philippine Archipelago or all
of Luzon. This is fortunate, for although the
fortifications on Corregidor deny entrance to
Manila Bay from the sea, Luzon is open to in-

vasion from Subig Bay and Lingayen Gulf on the west coast, from Lamon Bay on the east coast, and from Batangas Bay on the south coast. To defend its entire coast line would require many troops. Other factors favor the defense. Wind and weather conditions are rarely suitable for simultaneous landings on the east and west coasts, and along the roads to Manila from the beaches there are several difficult mountain passes and marshy areas that would enable a small force to delay the advance of the Japanese on Manila. Submarines, destroyers and aircraft from the Asiatic Fleet would assist the defenses of Corregidor. The American plan of defense of the Philippine Islands should have provided for this Manila Bay area fortifications sufficiently strong to hold out until the fleet could arrive from the Atlantic coast, plus a margin of safety. Since 1898 the United States has had many opportunities to prepare the Manila Bay area to resist a siege of any length up to a year. A properly fortified Manila would have given ample time for the United States Fleet to proceed in formation from any port on the Atlantic coast to Manila Bay.

When the defenses of Corregidor were constructed they were probably equal to any in the world. The restriction of the Naval Limitations Treaty and the uncertainty of the Philippines' political status have combined to prevent them from being continuously improved. They are still formidable and can resist a frontal attack by the Japanese Navy. How long they could resist a major attack from their rear is, like some other factors in the problem, uncertain. In preparation for their independence the Filipinos are raising an army under the direction of former Chief of Staff Gen. Douglas MacArthur; they have had little military experience, but under American direction and stiffened with American regulars MacArthur's Filipino divisions would be a welcome addition to the Manila Bay garrison.

In 1917 Maj. Gen. John F. Morrison, who knew the Philippines and every part of Luzon, estimated about 6,000 American Infantry, reenforced by Filipino Constabulary, with the garrison at Corregidor could hold the Manila Bay area as long as its military stores lasted. Since that time the defenses of Corregidor have become relatively weaker compared to the offensive weapons, guns and bombs that might be used against them; but the number of Filipinos trained for battle is larger, the defenses have been increased by detachments of submarines and the air force, and the American Army can provide many more than 6,000 infantry if necessary.

General Morrison knew the Japanese High Command of that decade well, having been a military observer during the Russo-Japanese War; he did not believe they would land an army in Luzon until they had captured Guam, for fear it would be cut off from Japan when the American Fleet arrived at Guam. Guam had another advantage: it was smaller than Luzon and could be held with fewer troops. Therefore General Morrison regarded it as more important than Luzon and recommended that it be properly fortified and its harbor facilities improved.

Mahan's study of naval strategy and the American position in the Far East convinced him that a navy able to defend the Monroe Doctrine and American interests abroad in other parts of the world would be sufficient to defend the political and commercial interests of the United States in the Far East. He did not, of course, believe that the United States could simultaneously defend all of its interests all over the world from all possible enemies. He did believe that by keeping the United States Fleet concentrated it could protect the interests in the most vital area, and return later to the less necessary areas. He knew that Great Britain had been forced to abandon various overseas possessions during her many wars, but by command of the sea she had eventually recovered most of them.

With particular reference to the Far East, Mahan was convinced that the size of the American naval force in that area would be determined not by the Philippines but by the most powerful enemy fleet. He believed the Philippines added to the value of American interests and, if provided with adequately equipped and fortified bases, would reduce the size of the naval force necessary to defend American lives and property in that area by providing for the refueling, refitting and repair of American ships.

Mahan concluded an essay on "Conditions Determining the Naval Expansion of the United States" with the statement that the conditions necessitating the creation of a powerful

American Navy were quite independent of the "relatively small external possessions"; the United States needed a navy because there was

a general movement of the nations . . . which seeks to secure commercial advantages in all quarters of the world; peaceably, if may be, but, if not, by pressure. In this collision of interests, force will have a determining part, as it has had in all periods of the world's history; and force, in such remote localities, means necessarily naval force. . . . Porto Rico, Hawaii, the Philippines . . . have not created the necessity; on the contrary, they have reduced the weight of the burden, by contributing [bases] to the support of it.[3]

In 1941 it is the collision of interests all over the world outlined in the beginning of this chapter and not the retention or independence of the Philippines that should determine the action of the United States in the Far East. That problem can be outlined by a few questions. Shall the United States permit Japan to gain exclusive control of the raw resources and markets of China, the Netherlands East Indies, and French Indo-China? If the United States is unwilling to permit that, would it be wiser

3. Alfred Thayer Mahan, *Retrospect and Prospect* (Boston, Little, Brown & Co., 1902), pp. 52, 53.

to take measures to stop Japan's advance now, while she is dependent primarily on the resources of her own islands, while her army is weary from its three-year struggle with China, while Great Britain, the Dutch East Indies and China can give assistance? If the United States permits Japan to expand, will she proceed to take Manila and Singapore and threaten Australasia? Answers to these questions would indicate the policy the United States should follow in the Far East.

With respect to their defense, the Philippines should be regarded as a valuable but not vital possession of the United States which, if the situation nearer home demanded it, could be temporarily evacuated. When the war was won their retrocession could be obtained without landing a soldier on them. If the defenses of Manila Bay were taken in hand and the garrison reënforced, temporary evacuation would be unnecessary, Luzon would be spared invasion and the navy would have operating bases which would reduce the total naval force required to defend its other interests in the Far East.

In accordance with its pledge the United States is taking the preliminary measures to transfer all authority to the Filipino Government which is preparing to accept its responsibilities. If the world situation becomes more threatening the Philippine Government may ask the United States to guarantee their independence in exchange for naval and air bases: this arrangement would of course be similar to the one made for bases in British possessions and it would be mutually advantageous if the United States could control the foreign policy of the Philippines. Such questions are for the future. The defense of the Philippines is a national obligation until they are formally given their independence.

When the Filipinos become independent, expenditures by the United States on the defenses of Luzon will be a financial loss, but they will justify their cost if the United States becomes involved in a war with Japan in the meantime. If the Philippine Government later on should offer bases to the United States in return for some form of protection, these expenditures would be recovered. Expenditures on Guam will be justified whether or not the Philippines are given their independence: if they are kept under our flag Guam will be their immediate support; if they become inde-

pendent the value of Guam to the United
States will greatly increase, because it will be-
come the most advanced base the United
States possesses in the Far East.

American interests in the Far East are often
disparaged but they were important before
the Philippines were acquired—they will be
important if we lose the Philippines. These interests were not fostered by subsidies from a
rich paternal government, nor did they spring
up overnight; their foundation was slowly and
painfully laid during the early days of the republic by the initiative, enterprise and persistence of American merchant mariners, who before the arrival of men-of-war defended themselves and their property with their own small
batteries from Malay and Chinese pirates. In
1820 the frigate *Congress* was sent to Manila
to assist in the protection of our merchantmen.
She was the forerunner of the United States
East Indies Squadron which in turn became
the Asiatic Squadron and Fleet. Dewey's ships
were on their regularly assigned station to protect American interests, as their predecessors
had been since 1820 and as their successors are
today, when he was ordered from Hong Kong
to destroy the Spanish Fleet in Manila. Acqui-

sition of the Philippines resulted from—it was not responsible for—American interests in the Far East. Today the Asiatic Fleet protects American trade from the aggressions of the Japanese Navy and Army.

Interests abroad produced the first favorable balance of American trade, and profits from the merchant marine and whalers made the industries of New England and the Middle States possible by providing needed capital; the merchant marine also provided raw materials (molasses to make Medford rum was a notable example), and a cheap carriage to markets. Deprived of their West Indian trade after the United States became independent, resourceful American mariners sailed into the Mediterranean Sea, around Cape Horn and the Cape of Good Hope into the Pacific and Indian oceans; many never returned, but other ships were building at home and eager young sailors were ready to man them. By 1812 the merchant marine of the United States was second only to the British; wherever cargo could be found a Yankee ship was there to bid for it. Entering the China trade via the Netherlands East Indies, American mariners were reveling in the lucrative Hong Kong trade when Japanese ships were restricted to their own waters; in 1837 the American ship *Morrison* trading from Portuguese Macao made a special voyage to Japan in the vain hope of opening commercial relations.

Since 1837 American commerce with the Far East, although fluctuating from time to time, has always formed a respectable portion of American foreign trade. In addition to their purely commercial trade in the western Pacific, Americans have established missions, colleges, hospitals and settlements throughout the region, especially in China. The wisdom of protecting these extensive interests has been challenged by the correct but incomplete statement that the entire American trade with China is less than the cost of a war with Japan; this statement is followed by the specious conclusion that economic considerations demand that the United States abandon its interests in the Far East lest they involve the nation in a war with Japan.

If the foregoing is a valid argument for abandoning American interests in the Far East, it applies with equal force to all American interests abroad and particularly to those in southern Brazil, Uruguay, Paraguay and

Argentina, which are as distant from the United States naval bases in the Atlantic as Manila is from Honolulu and would be as costly to defend against a European aggressor. To decide a question of war or peace on the immediate economic gain or loss is not only base, it is absurd. Only a war against an opulent and unarmed country will yield an immediate economic profit. It is necessary to take a longer view and consider other than immediate economic factors before passing judgment upon the proposed American withdrawal from the Far East.

If the United States withdrew immediately to the Aleutian, Hawaiian and Samoan Islands there would still be a Japanese-American frontier in the Pacific and it would still require protection. The expansive, trade-seeking Japanese would redouble their efforts to gain additional commercial privileges in Canada, Central and South America. Their exclusion from the United States would still rankle, their initial success in expelling the United States from the Far East would increase their determination to assert themselves, and the probability of war between Japan and the United States would increase. A war would then be fought

in the eastern Pacific and against a stronger
Japan. The Japanese have on file in Washington a protest against American possession of
the Hawaiian Islands. Their present government has recently suggested that the white race
evacuate all the South Sea Islands. It has compelled the French to cede to Thailand territory
held by France longer than the United States
has possessed the Hawaiian Islands. The Japanese population in Hawaii would provide a
sufficient pretext to revive the question of possession and the present Japanese Government
does not lack temerity. If the present generation of Americans yields the Philippines and
Guam to Japan, the next generation would
probably have to fight or yield parts of the
Aleutian and the Hawaiian Islands. Abandoning our position in China to placate Japan
may postpone but it will not avert a definite
trial of strength by all means short of, and perhaps including, the intervention of the armed
forces of Japan and the United States. And if
war comes it would be far better for the
United States to lose a naval campaign in the
Far East than to win a decisive victory over a
Japanese Expeditionary Force in California.

Before Great Britain became involved in the

present war the United States Fleet stationed in the Pacific offered sufficient protection to the Philippines and American territory in the western Pacific and the Atlantic. If Great Britain is defeated the United States will be obliged to create and maintain a two-ocean navy, the equivalent of the present British and American Fleets, to preserve our immediate interests against attacks from Germany, Italy, and Japan. A two-ocean navy would also provide for the defense of the Philippines. Under any and all circumstances a navy sufficiently strong to protect the Monroe Doctrine will also protect the open-door policy; if it can protect Argentina or Paraguay from an attack from Europe it can also protect the Philippine Islands from the Japanese. And as these same ships can be used in the Atlantic, their entire cost should not be charged to the Far East. Americans should not be deceived by the bland proposal of the Japanese Government to relieve them of their onerous and unprofitable task of protecting the Philippines and other possessions in the Far East.

The modern balance of power in the Far East was established from the balance of power existing in Europe, but it quickly became

strong enough to react upon its European pro-
genitor. Eurasian Russia, sprawling across Europe and Asia, linked the two systems by land;
the British Empire linked them by sea; the
parallel systems transmitted shocks almost instantaneously from one system to the other by
sea and land. The United States influences and
is influenced by both systems. The current balance of power in the Far East is mainly the result of the wars between Russia, Japan and
China. The influence of Great Britain has
been temporarily eliminated and that of the
United States has been cautiously applied.
The perennial struggle between Japan and
Russia for more Chinese territory is still in
progress, despite the Axis agreements and the
Russian-German understanding, and will continue unless China is able to drive out both invaders. China is slowly learning to fight the
hard way, by actual fighting; she has moved
her industries into the interior and constructed a road system throughout free China
while fighting; her leaders are confident they
can eventually drive Japan out of central
China and Manchuria, and regard the present
war as a unifying process worth its cost in Chinese blood and treasure. They may be over-

optimistic, but their stubborn resistance has surprised many observers and has prevented the Japanese from obtaining the economic advantages confidently anticipated.

While fighting China, Japan has been compelled to retain about a dozen of her best divisions, over 200,000 troops, in Manchukuo and North China, in readiness to meet the Soviet's Siberian Army. About 35 Japanese divisions, approximately 500,000 troops, have been employed against the Chinese Army in Central and South China. Japan can probably maintain at full strength between 55 and 60 divisions, so the bulk of the army has been absorbed in China and Manchukuo for over two years; its maintenance overseas has caused a shortage of man power in Japanese agriculture and industry at home. Realizing that since the collapse of France and the Low Countries greater opportunities beckon to the southwestward, the Japanese High Command is withdrawing divisions from China and concentrating them on Hainan Island, strategically placed to operate against Indo-China or any part of Malaya. As the troops have been withdrawn from China, the Chinese opposition in the remaining occupied areas has increased.

If the Japanese Army should become deeply
involved in the Netherlands East Indies and
Malaya, the Russian Army in Mongolia and
the maritime province of Siberia could use the
occasion to improve the Soviet's Siberian frontiers. The prolonged resistance of China and
the traditional hostility of Russia to Japan together have of course had an immediate effect
on the balance of power in the Far East and an
indirect effect on the world situation.

Japanese leaders may have been confused by
the rapid march of events; at any rate their recent diplomacy has lacked a little of its usual
deftness. The sudden agreement between Hitler and Stalin surprised the Japanese Foreign
Office and caused the resignation of the ministry that had formulated the anti-Comintern
pact. The governing class of Japan have seen
the Russian and the Chinese Empires transformed into a soviet and a republic. They fear
communism may spread among their industrial workers, and dread close relations with
the Soviet. It would be hazardous to permit
their war-weary soldiers in China to fraternize
with Stalin's proselyting Far Eastern Army.
But they cannot fully exploit the situation in
Malaya and risk a war with the United States

without a fundamental understanding with Russia.

The governments of Russia and Japan are opportunistic and would not let sentiment interfere with policy. Secretary Knox's proposal to neutralize the Manchurian railways in 1909 caused Japan and Russia temporarily to settle their differences and sign a secret treaty in 1910 to oppose the United States. If threatened by the same power they would jointly oppose it today. But a basis for a firm understanding between them does not exist. Russo-Japanese antagonism began in the 1870's; their interests momentarily coincided in 1910 but soon diverged. The strongest sentiment they have in common, an insatiable desire for more Chinese territory, only serves to perpetuate their rivalry. Russians and Japanese have fought so often that their nationals at home regard themselves as hereditary enemies. Japan confronts a future packed with dazzling possibilities, but also bristling with difficulties.

Vladivostok is the advance base of Stalin's Siberian forces, which he has made practically independent of supplies from European Russia by establishing munition factories in Asiatic Russia and the accumulation within its fortified zone of reserves of military and naval stores. Its strongly held and entrenched environs could withstand a Japanese siege by land and sea; within its military precincts are air fields and a naval base, whose planes and submarines would threaten any investing army or fleet. Vladivostok also happens to be the geographical center of the Japanese Empire; about equally distant from Port Arthur and Tokio, from Peiping and Shanghai. Every big city in industrial Japan and Japanese-occupied North China is within effective bombing distance of Vladivostok, and the sea communications of Japan with China would be exposed to Russian submarines and aircraft operating from that area.

The future policies of China and Russia will have an important influence on the outcome of a Japanese-American war. The United States has shown its appreciation of the indirect aid it has received through the Chinese resistance to Japan by lending China money and diplomatic support. If the United States went to war with Japan while the Chinese Army was still resisting the Japanese invaders, it could furnish the Chinese naval support, modern field artillery and aviation. With this material assistance and an American Army mission to advise the Chinese commanders, China could absorb more and more Japanese soldiers and might well cause a Japanese debacle comparable with Napoleon's retreat from Moscow. The Chinese leaders striving to make China independent of all foreign countries would not welcome the tutelage of the United States; but they know from experience that Americans do not desire Chinese territory or spheres of influence, only the right to trade on equal terms with all other foreigners doing business in China. China would coöperate with the United States in a war with Japan.

Russia and the United States have equally important reasons for opposing Japanese hegemony in China and the Far East; a joint Russo-American policy in the Far East could have halted the Japanese advance at any time during the past decade. The efforts of the Communists to spread their doctrines in the United States have made it impossible for Washington to coöperate with Moscow; and the failure of the United States to support its own Far Eastern policy vigorously has made the Kremlin doubt the value of American assistance. If the United States fortifies Guam and strengthens Manila, the Kremlin will have reason to assume that Washington is at last in earnest and may of its own accord and for its own purposes adopt a firmer attitude toward Japan.

The Kremlin will naturally be guided by its own interests in the event of Japanese-American hostilities; if the defeat of the United States, the leading capitalistic nation, was considered more desirable than the extension of Soviet territories, aid might be given to Japan. If the spread of communism was considered less appealing than an accession of territory, the Soviet would take advantage of the situation to attack Japan. With the German Army in force along her western frontier, Russia cannot afford to precipitate a war with Japan; but if the United States pressed Japan heavily, the Kremlin could find sufficient Soviet divisions to exploit the situation. Any Soviet action taken would follow the pattern of their European campaigns, half war—half peace. It would be unnecessary to persuade the Soviet to attack Japan if it was to her advantage, and it would be impossible to persuade her to attack Japan if it was not. However aroused and whatever form it took, Soviet hostility to Japan would assist the United States. And the American Fleet operating in the Pacific could not establish an effective long-range blockade of Japan if the Soviet undertook to nullify it by supplying Japan with essential materials. The surest way to gain the support of Russia and stop any assistance to Japan is to convince her by vigorous action that the United States can and will take care of its own interests.

War between Japan and the United States may arise over the immigration dispute, the open-door policy, or through the Japanese adherence to the Axis powers. These issues could fuse into one and they are all accentuated by Japanese industrial and commercial development which is in its infancy. Japanese industrialists have bought heavy machinery from Germany, Great Britain and the United States. They are expert copyists. They claim to have improved the textile machinery obtained from England. They have bought the latest developed steel rolling mills in the United States. Retaining their longer hours of labor and lower wages, with more efficient machinery and access to raw materials, the Japanese can produce goods much more cheaply than they do today.

The Japanese are also active competitors in deep-sea fisheries; they have developed floating factories by equipping large merchant ships to preserve and pack the daily catch of their steam fishing trawlers. These floating factories can make minor machinery repairs and provide fuel and supplies for a flotilla of trawlers, thus increasing their cruising radius and the time they can spend on the fishing grounds. By paying duty these steamers can deliver the canned fish to the American and Canadian markets before returning home, for they have extended their cruises to the waters off Alaska, Canada and Mexico.

Japanese shipbuilders can build merchant ships of all types cheaper than American builders; the cost of upkeep and maintenance is also less than ours. The salaries and wages of the officers and men are still under American standards, and the personnel of the merchant marine is comparable to the personnel of the navy in discipline. Nearly all the men are naval reserves with previous naval experience. Ship owners have no trouble with strikes, which are treated as mutinies. No American merchant ship can compete with a similar Japanese ship. The Japanese exporter can buy his goods cheaper at home and he can deliver them in any part of the world in Japanese bottoms at a fraction of the freight that an American ship operator would have to charge an American exporter. American textile manufacturers have felt Japanese competition for several years; every factory in the United States dependent upon foreign markets will feel it increasingly in the next decade, and the Japanese are making determined efforts to establish themselves in South America.

The question of immigration brought Japan and the United States to the brink of war in 1906, 1907 and 1913. It flared up again in 1924, when as a part of a comprehensive immigration law Congress provided for the "total exclusion of aliens ineligible to citizenship."[4] At present the issue is dormant, but in California or Arizona, where white farmers are in competition with Japanese farmers, the issue may become critical overnight. Some students

4. A. Whitney Griswold, *The Far Eastern Policy of the United States* (New York, Harcourt, Brace & Co., 1938), p. 374.

of Japanese-American affairs believe the Japanese born and reared in Hawaii and the United States will improve the relations between the two countries; others are equally confident that the Japanese are and will remain an unassimilable racial group among our citizenry.

The restriction on immigration will remain, because Americans west of the Rockies are determined to exclude any more Japanese; Southerners, with their own race problem, sympathize with the Westerners; members of labor unions and small farmers who actually meet the competition of Japanese laborers and farmers are resolved on exclusion; these groups combined are strong enough to prevent any change in the immigration law. The entire Japanese nation regards exclusion from the United States as a personal and national affront, for in spite of their pride in their achievements they realize that they are newcomers among the great nations, are self-conscious and more sensitive to slights real or imaginary, than Europeans and Americans. While the Japanese are irritated by their exclusion from the United States, Americans equally resent Japanese treatment of their countrymen in China. These two irritations are accentuated by commercial competition and at present by the general world situation.

No Japanese Government will accept the risk of war with the United States over the exclusion of immigrants unless compelled to by public opinion. Any government will accept it if the United States interposes between Japan and her territorial and commercial objectives in the Far East. The prospect of a German victory over Great Britain encouraged Japan to think that the United States would be so preoccupied with the situation in the Atlantic that the American Fleet would be withdrawn from the Pacific. She hastened to take advantage of this situation by announcing her adherence to the Axis powers. Japanese statesmen thought the long-awaited opportunity to secure their position in the Far East had arrived. But Germany's expected victory was delayed; the American Fleet remained in the Pacific; the Japanese Government has refrained from drastic action. When the Japanese High Command decide to go to war with the United States they will complete every possible preparation in advance, they will choose the time and place of attack, they will reduce the risks

to a minimum and boldly accept those remaining.

Whatever the cause of a war between Japan
and the United States, it would be fought in
the North Pacific. The Pacific, approximately
64,000,000 square miles, is almost as large as
the Atlantic and Indian oceans combined. In
the coastal waters of eastern Asia and western
North America the sea traffic is heavy but in
the middle reaches of the North Pacific a voy-
ager steaming along its regular trade routes
rarely sights a passing vessel. From Alaska, the
Aleutian Islands and the Hawaiian Islands,
the United States Fleet could control the entire North Pacific as far west as the international date line (180° east or west longitude);
while possession of the Kuril Islands, Formosa,
and the Pescadores Islands would enable the
Japanese Fleet to control the Sea of Japan, the
Yellow Sea, and the extreme northern part of
the China Sea, and assure her sea communications with Manchuria and North China.

Between these sea areas lies a middle zone
of almost unbroken sea, bordered on the south
by the Marshall and Caroline Islands, which
parallels the equator from 170° east longitude
to within 500 miles of the southern Philip-

pines, in which the control would be in dispute. The Marianas, running almost north and south, form stepping stones between the Caroline and the Bonin Islands, which are only 500 miles off the mainland of Japan. The Japanese chain which forms an irregular inverted "T" is broken by an American island, Guam, the southernmost of the Marianas, with a small but excellent natural harbor at Apra, which could be easily improved to accommodate several capital and numerous smaller ships.

Guam is 1,500 miles from Manila via the San Bernardino Strait, 1,453 miles to Shimonoseki at the western entrance of the Inland Sea, while Manila is 1,436 miles from Shimonoseki; Guam, Manila and Shimonoseki thus form an almost equilateral triangle with 1,500-mile sides. Guam lies a little south of the route from Honolulu to Manila, and going by way of it adds about 50 miles to the shortest distance, which is 4,767 miles. Guam is slightly more than two thirds of the distance from Honolulu to Manila and reduces the longest leg of the route from San Francisco to Manila from 4,767 to 3,318 miles. Guam's size, position and secure harbor combine to make it essential to the United States Navy. With a fleet speed of 12½ knots, the time at sea from Honolulu drops from almost 15 to a little more than 11 days; and numerous small vessels which could not reach Manila from Honolulu without refueling can steam the distance to Guam.

As has been noted Guam is much smaller than the island of Luzon, and can be defended with fewer soldiers, although it is in easy striking distance of Japan and almost surrounded by Japanese islets. Properly fortified it would be as strong as Malta, and would make an excellent advance base for the fleet. When the United States limited its navy in 1922 it agreed to refrain from strengthening or increasing the fortification of Guam or Manila. In 1936 Japan denounced that treaty; its provisions no longer restrict the United States.

A small string of islets connects north Luzon with south Formosa, off the southwest coast of which lie the Pescadores Islands, Japan's naval base nearest to Manila. The harbors of these islands are closed to foreigners, their defenses and facilities are not known; but from their hydrography it is probable that they can be used only as advance bases for cruisers, light forces and aircraft, and are not capable of sup-

porting capital ships. They would be exceed-
ingly useful to Japan in a campaign against the
Philippines. On the north extremity of Formosa is another small base, Keelung, capable
of handling any but capital ships. In the Luchu Islands, Amamio Shima has a spacious harbor, but its port facilities are not extensive.

In Japan the entire Inland Sea may be regarded as the main operating base for the Japanese Fleet. On its shores are Kobe and the
Kure Naval Base, and its hinterland includes
much of industrial Japan. For naval purposes
it is practically continuous with Yokohama
Bay, on which the Yokosuka naval station and
the ports of Tokio and Yokohama are situated.
Shimonoseki Straits give an exit to the Sea of
Japan on which is the Sasebo Naval Base; and
Bungo Strait and Kii Channel afford entrances
into the Pacific. It would be difficult to imagine a better natural base for a fleet than the Inland Sea, around whose coast the heavy industries of Japan are clustered. The Kuril Islands
extend the Japanese position to Kamchatka
and afford suitable bases for light forces to observe and report the approach of a naval force
from the Aleutian Islands. In their entirety
the Japanese islands stretch from the northern

end of Luzon almost to the western extremity of the Aleutians.

With all her strength, Japan labors under the inescapable disadvantage of being an insular, industrialized, densely populated nation. She is dependent upon the sea for her life. It is not necessary to invade Japan if her main trade routes to China and Manchukuo, to the United States and South America, to Europe and Australasia can be cut. The American Fleet based at Honolulu would automatically prevent all trade with North or South America. If it were based on the Philippines it would also cut off all trade with Europe and Australasia. This would leave only the sea route to China open; Japan could be completely isolated if that were closed by some form of distant blockade.

The western Pacific is a region well designed by nature for the rigorous employment of sea and air power. It will serve equally well the naval power of Japan or of the United States. If Japan should establish herself in Malaya, she would be almost invulnerable, and could dominate the Far East. If the American Fleet was securely established in Luzon and supported by army and navy aviation, Japan could still maintain herself at home but could no longer aspire to hegemony over the Far East. In few parts of the world are there three positions as strategically important as Guam, Luzon and Singapore. If these continue to be held by the United States and Great Britain, the status quo in the Far East can be maintained. If they are lost, Japan will dominate the Far East, threaten Australia and New Zealand and force the United States to fall back to Honolulu.

American army and navy opinion of the measures necessary to hold the Philippines as a base of operations has varied widely at different times. The immediate tactical problem is easy to state: when the American Fleet is absent from the Philippines, can the army hold Manila Bay until the fleet arrives, with or without reënforcements for the army, sufficiently strong to drive off a blockading fleet and prepared to cut the communications of an enemy army in Luzon? The problem resembles that of Port Arthur in 1904–5, except that the American Army is alert, the Russians were inert; the American Fleet is concentrated, the Russian was divided; and the American Fleet

is nearer to the theater of operations than Rojestvensky's Baltic Squadron.

If the United States Army were forced to
surrender Manila Bay before the fleet arrived,
the fleet would be compelled at the end of a
long voyage to seek a temporary base in the
southern Philippines, where numerous an-
chorages are available to refuel, refit and repair. It would probably suffer some losses en
route to Manila; it might suffer heavily but it
would also inflict loss and probably would still
be superior to the Japanese Fleet. If so, the
Japanese Fleet would either have to fight or to
abandon its army in Luzon. If the American
Fleet were reduced below the strength of the
opposing fleet it would have to refuel and return to Hawaii.

No general can guarantee to hold a fort a
certain number of days, no admiral can guarantee to arrive with the fleet by a certain date;
responsible officers can only give assurances
that they will use their utmost endeavors. The
rest must be left to the fortunes of war. The
defense of the Philippines under existing circumstances is one of the doubtful problems
that often confronts Commanders in Chief in

wartime, but the odds are decidedly in favor of the United States. And even if the Japanese succeeded in occupying the Philippines, unless they decisively defeated our fleet their tenure would be short, for those islands will eventually go to the nation that controls the sea.

The relative strengths of the Japanese and American Fleets may be approximately placed at 70 to 100. If the American Fleet happened to be in the Manila area when hostilities occurred, there would be no siege of Manila and no Japanese troops landed on Luzon, unless the Japanese Fleet could defeat the American. Based on Manila, the American Fleet could obtain its fuel from the Netherlands East Indies, its food from Australia, and would be dependent upon the United States only for replacement of personnel and munitions. Its position would automatically protect practically all its own lines of communications.

Operating from the Manila area, the American Fleet would be exposed to attacks by Japanese submarines and aircraft; the Japanese Fleet would also be exposed to American submarines and naval aviation plus some army aviation. If Japan resorted to unrestricted submarine warfare American submarines could retaliate. If Japan delayed a fleet action and waged a war of attrition, American cruisers, destroyers, submarines and planes could probably inflict as much damage on the Japanese Fleet as the American Fleet would receive. If the Japanese depended upon cruiser warfare against merchantmen, our 8-inch cruisers (described in Chapter V) can do fully as much harm to Japanese shipping, and Japan is more dependent upon her shipping than is the United States. If the Japanese preferred to settle the war by a decisive day engagement somewhere in the South China Sea the American Fleet would welcome the opportunity. On account of the distance from bases to the battlefield, ships of both sides badly damaged under water in an engagement in the South China Sea would probably be sunk; the American Fleet can accept losses provided it is able to inflict them.

Under existing circumstances Australasia would refuse to trade with Japan if she were at war with the United States. American cruisers based on home ports would interrupt all Japanese trade with South America, leaving the Japanese islands dependent solely upon their trade with Japanese-dominated China

and Siberia. Unless the fleets of the Axis powers threatened to gain control of the Atlantic,
the American Fleet could remain in the Far
East indefinitely, gradually tightening the
long-range blockade of Japan until her already
strained industrial-economic system collapsed.

When Gen. U. S. Grant was marching
toward the Confederate Army near Belmont,
Missouri, he tormented himself with apprehensions of what the Confederates could do to
his regiment; suddenly he thought of what his
force could do to the Confederates. At that
point his fears vanished and he won his first
victory of the Civil War. Many Americans have
overestimated Japan and underestimated their
own military power. They might follow
Grant's example and consider what they can
do to Japan. Sober calculation should convince them that their apprehensions have no
substantial basis, and they can decide upon
their policy in the Far East calmly and justly,
without basing it upon their fears.

CHAPTER FIVE

THE JAPANESE AND AMERICAN NAVIES

DURING a war between the United States and Japan the invasion of either country by the army of the other would be practically impossible. The opposing armies would have important but secondary tasks: the Japanese might invade Luzon, the American Army would garrison overseas bases and its aviation coöperate with the Navy. The final outcome of the war would be determined by the operations of the two fleets, which include submarines, naval aviation and all available army aviation. Both fleets would endeavor to gain and exercise control of the western Pacific to insure its use to friendly ships and deny it to hostile ones. The quickest way to obtain this control is to defeat the opposing fleet.

The Commander in Chief of the American Fleet, which is the stronger,[1] would endeavor

1. We are assuming here, as will be explained in the next chapter, that the three American Fleets will operate as a

to bring the Japanese Fleet to action in the open sea; the Commander in Chief of the Japanese Fleet would probably be unwilling to engage the American Fleet except in an area where coastal submarines, land-based aviation and mine fields could compensate for the weakness in other branches, particularly in the battle line. The Japanese Commander in Chief would probably endeavor to reduce the American superiority by submarines, aviation and mine fields before accepting a daylight action in which he would risk defeat and possible annihilation. He would attempt a war of attrition as soon as hostilities commence, and would take full advantage of Japan's geographical position to wage it. Whether the initial American superiority could be reduced would depend upon the relative skill of the opposing personnel, the margin of initial superiority, and the capacity of the heavy industries of the two nations to replace ships and the two Navy Departments to supply personnel. A comparison of the personnel and ships of the American and Japanese Navies will assist in forecasting the course of the war.

unit. It should be noted also that the fleets of possible allies are omitted.

Japanese flag officers and naval captains are younger on the average than the American, and are correspondingly better able to withstand the physical strain of a campaign. Farragut was an old officer when he distinguished himself, and his illustrious career may be offered to justify old commanders; but he was obliged to leave his command in the Gulf of Mexico on account of illness and during his absence important operations were delayed. The Japanese have a distinct advantage in their younger fleet commanders. In the intermediate grades the Japanese are also younger; and only the midshipmen and ensigns of the two navies are of about equal age.

American officers are required to perform both line and engineering duties, while the Japanese have a separate corps of engineer officers. The Americans have more sea experience and as they are promoted less rapidly should be more familiar with their duties. Japanese officers as a rule work harder and take less recreation; they are permitted less initiative and must wait longer for orders. The officers of both fleets are alert, well trained and accustomed to the sea; they are equally proficient and scrupulous in the execution of routine duties and would be well matched in courage. In professional attainments, American officers would probably average higher. An Imperial precept to the Japanese Army and Navy charges them to "bear in mind that duty is weightier than a mountain, while death is lighter than a feather." Togo before the battle of Tsushima, in an order of the day, told his fleet, "a positive attack is the best form of defense"—unconsciously paraphrasing Farragut and Mahan. The officers and men of the Japanese Army and Navy have shown on the battlefield that they are inspired by the precepts of their Emperor and Admiral Togo. The United States Navy created and is inspired by its own traditions; they are revealed in Paul Jones's "We have just commenced to fight," Farragut's "Damn the torpedoes! Go ahead!" and Dewey's matter-of-fact "You may fire when ready, Gridley." But naval traditions are bequeathed by example rather than precept and in the annals of both services can be found warrant for the faith each country has in its navy.

The enlisted personnel of the Japanese Navy are older and perhaps a little better schooled in their duties, for they remain longer on a particular position than American sailors, who are usually promoted more rapidly because of the turnover in personnel in the United States Navy. The American enlisted personnel are quicker mentally and would probably react more promptly to an unexpected situation. The crews of both services are deep-sea sailors and could fight in any part of the world, although the Americans have usually cruised greater distances, for the Japanese Fleet rarely leaves its home waters. The Japanese are more accustomed to winter cruising in northern latitudes; the American sailors spend much time in the milder climates of southern California and the tropics. The physical condition of officers and men of both fleets is very good, their morale is high, they will cheerfully endure the burdens of a long campaign and, if it culminates in a decisive naval engagement, they will be equal to the ordeal of the battle.

A comparative analysis of the various categories of Japanese and American ships establishes the margin of initial material superiority enjoyed by the United States Navy. Until Japan withdrew from the Naval Conference in 1936 the numbers, displacement, speed, armor and armament of all types of ships of the two navies were known; since 1936 it has been increasingly difficult to obtain data on Japanese ships. Some naval information has been published in Japan. The annual capacity of her shipyards, which is increasing, can be estimated and it is not easy even in Japan to conceal a cruiser, aircraft carrier or battleship. Naval publications in various countries, such as the *United States Naval Institute Proceedings,* the British *United Service Institution, Brassey's Naval Annual,* and *Jane's Fighting Ships,* take considerable pains to ascertain the relative strength of the leading navies. In this present analysis the comparative data on armor, armament, speed, dimensions and other characteristics of American and Japanese ships are obtained from these publications, and not from official sources—with the exception of press releases by the United States Navy Department.[2]

The information service of the Navy Department issued the following comparative

2. The most prolific source of information on the United States Navy is the *Congressional Record,* which publishes practically all reports furnished Congress by the Navy Department; it is carefully scanned by every naval attaché stationed in Washington.

table of the Japanese and American Navies on March 1, 1941, but did not guarantee the Japanese data.

The Numerical Strength of the Japanese and American Navies.[3]

TYPE	JAPAN	UNITED STATES	JAPAN	UNITED STATES
	Built		Building	
Battleships	10*	15†	8‡	17
Aircraft Carriers	8	6	2	12
Cruisers	46	37	10	54
Destroyers	125	160§	11	204
Submarines	71	105	7	80
	260	323	38	367

* Includes the *Hi Yei* which was demilitarized but is reported to have been remilitarized.

† Does not include the *Wyoming,* which has been demilitarized and is suitable for training purposes only.

‡ Estimated.

§ Does not include 50 over-age destroyers traded to Great Britain.

The figures given by the Navy Department can be accepted for the United States Navy. Those given for Japan have been independently checked by adding to the ships Japan possessed in 1937, which were accurately known,

3. Authority: Navy Department, Washington. Official *Press Release.*

those probably completed since that date, using data derived from sources already mentioned and *The Japan Year Book* which until recently contained detailed information of Japanese ships. Few comparisons are exactly alike, as different standards of obsolescence are applied; and there is no assurance that the figures given are exact to the last ship or gun. The figures for battleships, aircraft carriers and cruisers given hereafter may be more exact than those for destroyers and submarines.

The relative strengths of the opposing battle lines have been the determining factor in naval campaigns of the nineteenth and twentieth centuries. Five superdreadnaughts transferred from Great Britain to Germany in 1914 would have made the British blockade impossible. The power of aviation is increasing, but events of the current war indicate that the strength of the battle line is still the decisive naval factor. Battleships have two characteristics of a heavyweight boxing champion, the ability to give and take terrific blows. They can withstand several direct hits by major caliber bombs, two or perhaps more underwater hits by torpedoes, and several direct hits by 16-inch or 14-inch armor-piercing shells. They can sustain more damage than ships of any other type, whether from bombs, torpedoes or heavy projectiles, and continue to fight, for they are almost unsinkable. Under average conditions a battleship would begin an engagement with about 1,200 heavy projectiles; it would require 1,200 bombing planes to carry in a single flight 1,200 1-ton bombs, which are comparable in destructive power. As planes improve this ratio will decrease, but when planes can carry 3 1-ton bombs it will still take 400 planes to equal a single battleship in hitting power for the duration of an engagement.

Japan has 2 battleships with 16-inch guns, the *Mutsu* and *Nagato;* the United States has 3, the *Colorado, West Virginia* and *Maryland.* These battleships are the peers of any ships afloat except the British *King George VI* class and the new American *North Carolinas.* All carry 8 16-inch guns in 4 turrets; their displacement is about the same—32,000 tons. The Japanese are 700 feet long, the American 624, with approximately the same beam, 97½ feet, and draught, 30–35 feet. The Japanese are faster: their original speed was 23.5 knots, that of the American 22. Since they have been modernized and reboilered, the Japanese ships are reported to make 26 knots while the American can make about 21 knots at present.

The main armor belts of the Japanese ships are 14 inches thick around the turrets and 12 around the conning towers, from 13 to 9 inches around the midship area, including machinery spaces and magazines, and taper to 8 and 4 inches at the bow and stern; the armored decks are 3½ inches. American ships have 16- to 18-inch armor around the turrets and conning towers, midship belts of 16 to 14 inches tapering to 8 inches at the bow and stern, and 3-inch armored decks. Both American and Japanese battleships are protected from air bombs by armored decks and divided by horizontal and vertical bulkheads into compartments that serve to localize any injury. It is the cellular interiors resembling steel honeycombs which make modern battleships almost unsinkable. If battered into helpless hulks, they would probably still float. The *Warspite* was repeatedly hit by major caliber German shells and the *Marlborough* was torpedoed during Jutland, but both continued to fight. Present-day battleships are even stronger and would survive numerous hits at battle ranges.

Japan has 4 battleships armed with 12 14-

inch guns: *Fuso, Hyuga, Ise* and *Yamashiro.*
The United States has 7: *Arizona, California,*
Idaho, Mississippi, New Mexico, Pennsylvania
and *Tennessee.* Japan has converted 3 battle
cruisers, *Haruna, Kirishima* and *Kongo,* into
fast battleships by increasing their compart-
mentation and armor. It was not feasible to increase their battery. They are faster than corresponding American battleships but carry less
armor (10 to 3 inch) and fewer guns. The *Hi*
Yei, a sister of the *Kongo,* was demilitarized
like the *Wyoming;* it is reported that she has
again been militarized; if so, it is very doubtful
that her former strength could be restored.
With the *Hi Yei,* the Japanese would have
4 battleships carrying 8 14-inch guns; the
United States has 4, the *Nevada, Oklahoma,*
Texas and *New York,* carrying 10 14-inch
guns. Japan would thus have 8 14-inch gun
battleships with a total of 80 14-inch guns; the
United States 11 with a total of 124 14-inch
guns, to which could be added the *Arkansas*
with 12 12-inch guns.

The defensive batteries of both Japanese
and American battleships for use against destroyers, submarines and aircraft are approximately equal, consisting of 6-, 5- and 3-inch

guns; the Japanese generally use 6- and the American 5-inch guns against destroyers; both use 3- and 5-inch antiaircraft guns.

American battleships average a year or two younger than the Japanese, but all the Japanese have been reconditioned, while 5 of the American have not. While the 14-inch gun battleships of the Japanese are faster, the American have more guns and heavier armor.

Numerical superiority in battleships is difficult to overcome. There are not only more guns that inflict damage but fewer enemy ships to be destroyed or disabled before victory is assured. The odds in favor of a fleet of 10 against 7 sister ships are 100 to 49 at the beginning of an engagement. As the superior fleet should inflict increasing damage with each salvo, the ratio would gradually rise to the cube of the number of ships engaged and the ratio of 10 ships to 7 toward the end of an engagement should increase to 1,000 to 343. Assuming equality of personnel in an engagement with all ships present on a day of high visibility, the American battle line with its 24 16-inch guns plus 124 14-inch guns in 14 ships opposed to 16 16-inch guns plus 80 14-inch in 10 ships should decisively defeat the Japanese battle line.

Comparison of Japanese and American Battle Lines

JAPANESE

Class	Speed	Armor	Guns
2 *Nagatos*	23–26 knots	14–3½ inches	8 16-in.
4 *Fusos*	22–23	12–4	12 14-in.
3 *Kongos*	26	10–3	8 14-in.

9 battleships	16 16-in. guns
	72 14-in. guns

AMERICAN

Class	Speed	Armor	Guns
3 *West Virginias*	20–21 knots	18–3 inches	8 16-in.
7 *Californias*	21	18–3	12 14-in.
4 *Nevadas*	20–21	18–3	10 14-in.
1 *Arkansas*	18–20	12–3	12 12-in.

15 battleships	24 16-in. guns
	124 14-in. guns
	12 12-in. guns

Demilitarized

JAPANESE	AMERICAN
Hi Yei (*Kongo* class) reported refitted for service, but this would be difficult to accomplish.	*Wyoming* (*Arkansas* class) used for training purposes.

The Japanese *Hosho* and the American *Langley*, the first aircraft carriers in either navy, were built about the same time (1921–22), but the *Hosho* was faster and carried

more planes. The *Langley* is assigned to the
Asiatic Fleet but is considered obsolete, while
the Japanese still retain the *Hosho* in service.
Japan has 2 27,000-ton carriers, the *Akagi,* a
converted battle cruiser, and the *Kaga,* a converted battleship, with speeds of 28.5 and 23
knots respectively. They were completed about
the same time as the American *Lexington* and
Saratoga, 33,000-ton carriers making 33 knots.
According to Brassey the two American carriers together have a capacity of 160 planes
against 110 for the two Japanese. The Japanese *Ryujo,* completed in 1933, displaces only
7,100 tons and carries 24 planes; the American
Ranger, completed a year later, is 14,500 tons
and carries 76 planes. The Japanese *Soryu,*
Hiryu and *Koryu* are sister ships of 10,050
tons, speed 30 knots and carry 40 aircraft each;
they are contemporary with but have only half
the displacement of the 20,000-ton American
Yorktown, Enterprise and *Hornet* which were
designed for a speed of 34 knots and capacity of 76 aircraft each. The American *Wasp*
(14,700 tons) has the same plane capacity. As a
group the American carriers are larger, speed-
ier, and carry more planes than the Japanese.

Japanese and American Aircraft Carriers

JAPANESE

Class	Speed	Planes	Guns
2 *Akagis*	23–28.5 knots	50–60	10 8-in.
			12 4.7-in. A.A.
1 *Ryujo*	25	24	12 5-in. A.A.
3 *Soryus*	30	40	12 5-in. A.A.
1 *Hosho*	25	26	4 5.5-in.
			2 3-in. A.A.

7 carriers*   280 planes

* The Navy Department credits Japan with 8 aircraft carriers in February 1941. She had 7 built or building in November 1937 when the *Koryu* (now known as the *Syokaku*) was laid down. It is not known whether she laid down any in 1938—the need for other types is greater—but in any case a carrier begun in 1938 would probably not be completed until well on in 1941 or early 1942, as sister ships required over three years to complete. Jane (1940) predicts that 2 carriers may be completed in 1941.

Building

2 or 3

AMERICAN

Class	Speed	Planes	Guns
2 *Lexingtons*	33 knots	80	8 8-in.
			12 5-in. A.A.
1 *Ranger*	29.5	76	8 5-in. A.A.
2 *Yorktowns*	34	76	8 5-in. A.A.
1 *Wasp*	30	77	8 5-in. A.A.

6 carriers   465 planes

Building

12 (including *Hornet*)

Aircraft carriers are as vulnerable as they are valuable; it is very difficult to protect their flying decks from determined attacks by enemy bombing planes or from salvos of heavy projectiles. Their position in the fleet cruising formation and after deployment for battle will be a perplexing problem to be determined by the particular circumstances existing when the decision is made. Both navies have devoted much thought to the question but it is doubtful if a consensus of opinion exists in either service. In addition to their use with the fleet, aircraft carriers strongly supported by either fast battleships or heavy cruisers will certainly be employed on independent missions.

The Japanese have five seaplane tenders, the *Kamoi, Notoro, Chitose, Chioda* and *Mizuo.* These mother ships are not provided with a flight deck. They carry planes on deck that can be catapulted into the air or hoisted over the side into the water, and other planes disassembled and crated in their holds. They proceed where needed, prepared to repair and service their planes. During the present Sino-Japanese War these ships have serviced and supplied most of the planes employed against the Chinese coast cities and armies. These mobile hangars would be very useful in the harbors of

the mandated islands, along the Chinese coasts
and at Japanese bases during a Japanese-
American war. On account of the islands that
form stepping stones from Japan, Formosa,
the Kuril, Bonin, Mariana, Caroline and Marshall Islands, this type of aircraft mother ship
is especially suitable to Japanese naval aviation needs. This prompted the government to
propose the abolition of aircraft carriers
equipped with flight decks. In the base force of
the American Pacific and Atlantic Fleets are
mother ships and seagoing tugs that accompany squadrons of flying boats to ports in the
Caribbean Sea, the Aleutian and Philippine
Islands where regular facilities for servicing
them are not available.

On paper Japan has available for service 44
cruisers, the United States 37. Included among
the Japanese are 5 armored and 2 light cruisers
built between 1899 and 1902. The United
States Navy considered obsolete and scrapped
10 armored and 3 light cruisers equal in all respects to these Japanese cruisers, which could
destroy any lone merchantman they overhaul,
but could not fight a modern cruiser, for their
guns are outranged, their armor insufficient

and their nominal speeds of 16 to 26 knots would not enable them to escape. Among the Japanese cruisers are 2 former Chinese ships, *Ning Hai* and *Ping Hai,* which were captured in 1937 and refitted in Japan. Completed in 1936, they displace 2,500 tons, carry 6 5.5-inch guns, 4 21-inch torpedo tubes, and 1 plane. They are a hybrid type, really fast gunboats, modern and useful, but not large enough for cruiser duty.

The *Tatuta, Tenryu* and *Yubari,* frequently listed as cruisers, are actually fast mine layers and will not be available for duty as cruisers; they displace about 3,000 tons and can make 31 to 33 knots. The United States Navy has fitted 8 of its 1,200-ton destroyers to serve as fast mine layers. Theoretically these ships can deny certain areas to an enemy fleet during action by laying mine fields; but the area of a naval battle is extensive, the number of mines carried is limited, fleets move rapidly, and the value of mine laying during a fleet action is doubtful. Tactically a mine is an immobile torpedo; it is effective in narrow fairways where ships must conform to the channel or run aground. Mine fields in other places can be avoided, unless planted on the scale of the

Anglo-American mine field in the North Sea during the last war. Narrow channels and fairways must be regularly swept before being used by valuable ships.

When obsolete and special type cruisers are eliminated, Japan has 32 ships available for regular cruiser duties and the United States 37.

Japanese and American Cruisers

JAPANESE			
Class	*Guns*	*Speed*	*Displacement*
8 *Myokos* and			
Nachis	10 8-in.	33 knots	10,000 tons
4 *Furutakas*	6 8-in.	33	7,100
6 *Mogamis*	12–15 6-in.	33	8,500
14 *Natoris*	7 5.5-in.	33	5,170
32 cruisers	104 8-in. guns		
	84 6-in. guns		
	98 5.5-in. guns		

AMERICAN			
Class	*Guns*	*Speed*	*Dis-placement*
2 *Pensacolas*			
6 *Northamptons*			9,000–
18 { 2 *Portlands*	9–10 8-in.	32–33 knots	10,000 tons
7 *Minneapolis*			
1 *Wichita*			
9 *Brooklyns*	15 6-in.	32.5	10,000
10 *Omahas*	10–12 6-in.	32–33	7,050
37 cruisers	164 8-in. guns		
	245 6-in. guns		

In heavy cruisers the United States has a decided superiority of 18 to 12. Neither navy possesses battle cruisers. Japan converted three battle cruisers, *Haruna, Kirishima,* and *Kongo,* into fast battleships. These 8-inch gun cruisers would be employed as distant scouts for the fleet or on independent duties, running down enemy raiders and attacking enemy merchant marine, or escorting important convoys. The modern 8-inch gun is a powerful weapon, but the cruisers are lightly armored compared with battleships and are not fit for the battle line. However, the Japanese employed their armored cruisers in the battle line at Tsushima, and it is possible they may again to compensate for their lack of battleships. If they do, these cruisers will not last as long as Fisher's "ten-minute" battle cruisers at Jutland. The British have found heavy cruisers very useful in the Mediterranean both in protecting their own and in attacking the Italian communications. These ships are well adapted to escort fast aircraft carriers making air raids.

Of cruisers operating with the fleet, scouting, screening or serving as flagships of destroyer squadrons, Japan has 20, the United States 19 of practically the same tactical char-

acteristics except that the 10 *Omahas* are larger
and more heavily armed than the 14 *Natoris*.
The 6 *Mogamis* are individually equivalent to
the 9 American *Brooklyn* class.

Light cruisers generally accompany the battle line and link it with its destroyers. In a
cruising formation, they shield the battle fleet
from inquisitive enemy surface scouts and insure the battle line against a tactical surprise
by day or destroyer attack by night. Preliminary to an engagement, they are employed to
obtain information of the enemy formation,
course and speed, and deny similar information of their fleet to the enemy. In a day or
night action they would endeavor to break
through an enemy defensive screen, to facilitate an attack by their destroyers, and would
attempt to repel similar attacks by enemy destroyers. The speed of cruisers and destroyers
is over 30 knots. Their maneuvers are kaleido-
scopic, tactical situations change in the twin-
kling of an eye, and a commander of the light
forces must react instantaneously to the rapidly changing situation.

Commodore (afterward Admiral) Goodenough commanded a division of Beatty's light
cruisers during the opening of the battle of

Jutland. He gave Beatty timely information of the approach of Scheer's battleships, and then maintained his position on the bow of the advancing German battle line, zigzagging to avoid its gunfire, and reported its continuously changing position to Jellicoe and Beatty. Goodenough gave an excellent example of the proper employment of light cruisers in a day action. The legendary account of Jutland asserts that Goodenough, whose ships were under continuous fire from the leading German battleships, steamed directly for the mean point of impact of the nearest German salvo, reasoning that the succeeding salvo would probably not fall in the same danger space.

Destroyers evolved from torpedo boats in the same manner that superdreadnaughts evolved from predreadnaughts and dreadnaughts. They surpass torpedo boats in size, speed and armament. They were originally designed as a defensive weapon to protect battleships and cruisers from torpedo boats. It became apparent that a destroyer was also an improved torpedo boat and could be advantageously used against enemy battleships and cruisers. The first torpedo boats displaced 200 to 400 tons; destroyer leaders, the largest of the torpedo-boat class today, displace around 2,000 tons. As small cruisers range from 3,000 to 4,000 tons, destroyer leaders can be considered either overgrown destroyers or undersized cruisers.

Destroyers are used offensively and defensively, day and night, and no unit commander in the fleet ever has enough of them. They are usually designed in classes of four or more sister ships. Prior to 1914, it was generally accepted that four destroyers were necessary for each battleship. That ratio has increased with the improvement of the submarine and airplane, and the battleship building "holiday"; today Japan has 14 destroyers, the United States 10.4 for each battleship.

The primary weapon of torpedo boats and destroyers is still the torpedo, although the original destroyers were more heavily armed than torpedo boats, in order to destroy the latter with gunfire. As the number of torpedo boats and destroyers increased, it became obvious that before they could reach a favorable position to launch their missiles they would have to fight their way through screens of opposing destroyers or cruisers. Accordingly the batteries of destroyers were gradually increased from guns firing 12-pound projectiles to those firing projectiles weighing from 32 to 50 pounds.

In 1917 and 1918 the United States Navy concentrated the nation's building facilities on destroyers, to meet the German submarine menace; by 1921 it possessed more modern destroyers than any other navy. Of these 74 are still in service on destroyer duties; some have been converted into fast mine layers, others are used on special duties such as plane guards for aircraft carriers.

Between 1920 and 1932 the United States did not lay down any destroyers. The Japanese built about 60, all more modern than the existing American ships. In 1932 the United States Navy laid down the *Farragut* class and by March 1, 1941, had completed 86 modern destroyers and destroyer leaders. It now has, under the two-ocean-navy program, 204 destroyers building or ordered, all of 1,500 tons or more, which can be finished at a rapid rate, for our shipyards are equipped for quantity production of destroyers. Japan had only 11 under construction when the two-ocean program was announced. Doubtless she will increase this number, but she cannot equal the destroyer program of the United States.

It is difficult to compare the military value of particular destroyers, for they serve many different purposes. Maneuverability, speed, and number of depth charges carried are the most valuable characteristics in operating against submarines; maneuverability, speed and gun power when operating against other destroyers; speed, maneuverability, number of torpedo tubes when operating against battleships. Destroyers become obsolete more rapidly than battleships or cruisers but when age renders them unfit for fleet duty they are still useful to escort convoys.

Of the destroyers built before 1925 still on the active list Japan has 53: 29 of 850 tons or under and 24 of 1,200 to 1,300 tons displacement; the United States has 74 of 1,200 tons. All these destroyers have been maintained in good operating condition, are serviceable and useful; they range from 15 to 24 years of age, and are not equal to the newer destroyers of either navy. In addition to the numerical superiority, each American destroyer of this group carries 4 triple torpedo tubes against 2 triple or 3 double torpedo tubes for the Japanese. Without having to reload, the American destroyer could fire a salvo of 12 torpedoes to 6 for the Japanese. In gun power the Japanese destroyers are individually superior: the American destroyer carries 4 4-inch guns against 3 or 4 4.7-inch guns for the Japanese. When new the speed of the American destroyers was 35 knots, the Japanese 31.5 to 34 knots. These speeds have since been reduced.

Since 1925 Japan has built 73, the United States 86 destroyers. They represent the latest tactical ideas of the two navies and are the best their constructors could build. The Japanese ships are usually smaller, 3 knots slower and carry fewer torpedo tubes. The dimensions of the 23 *Hubukis,* the largest Japanese destroyers, are: length over-all 371.5 feet, beam 34 feet, draught 10.7, standard displacement without ammunition, fuel or stores 1,700 tons. The dimensions of 13 *Somers* and *Porters,* the largest American destroyers, are: length over-all 381, beam 36.5, draught 10.3 feet, standard displacement 1,850. When fully loaded the Japanese displace 2,125 tons, the American around 2,275 tons. The *Hubukis* have 9 21-inch torpedo tubes and 6 5-inch guns; 8 *Porters* have 8 21-inch torpedo tubes, the 5 *Somers* have 12 torpedo tubes; and both carry 8 5-inch guns. The latest Japanese design, the *Kageros,* with a standard displacement of 1,500 tons carry 6 5-inch guns, 8 21-inch torpedo tubes, speed 34 knots; the latest American design, the *Bensons,* with a displacement of 1,630 tons carry 6 5-inch guns, 10 21-inch torpedo tubes and make 37 knots.

This comparison of destroyers and the following table are calculated on the assumption that 74 American ships completed prior to 1924 are available after exchanging 50 with Great Britain for naval and air bases, that all American destroyers through the *Sims* class and 13 of the *Benson* class are completed, and that all Japanese destroyers through the *Kagero* class laid down in 1937–38 are completed. Brassey and Jane differ from the estimate of the Navy Department by a few destroyers; they are unofficial British publications but furnish an excellent check on figures from American sources. In all probability a few more destroyers have been completed for both navies, but the relative position has not changed materially. Any change would probably favor the United States with its enlarged building program.

Comparison of Japanese and American Destroyers

JAPANESE

Class	Displacement	Completed
53 *Momo* to *Kamikaze* types	850 to 1,300 tons	Prior to 1925
12 *Mutukis*	1,300	1925–27
23 *Hubukis*	1,700	1927–32
6 *Hatuharus*	1,370	1933–35
10 *Sigures*	1,370	1935–36
10 *Asasios*	1,370	1937–38
12 *Kageros*	1,500	1939–40

126 completed

Japan has 12 modern torpedo boats built since 1933, displacing between 500 and 600 tons, speed 25 to 28 knots, carrying 2 or 3 21-in. torpedo tubes; and 8 are building. These small ships can be serviceable only in coastal waters; one of the first designed, the *Tomozuru*, capsized in 1934, but was repaired and is again in commission. There are at least 11 destroyers under construction.

AMERICAN

Class	Displacement	Completed
74 *Decaturs*	1,200 tons	Prior to 1925
8 *Farraguts*	1,400	1934–35
16 *Mahans*	1,500	1936–37
8 *Porters*	1,850	
5 *Somers*	1,850	1938–39
2 *Dunlaps*	1,500	1938
22 *Cravens*	1,500	1938–39
12 *Sims*	1,570	1939–40
13 *Bensons* completed	1,630	
(11 under construction)		

160 completed

The Navy Department announced that 204 destroyers were under construction March 1, 1941. This figure probably included 11 of the 24 *Bensons*, 13 having been completed. In addition to these 160 destroyers the United States has 8 of the 1,200-ton class equipped as fast mine layers, and a few others used as plane guards.

During the last World War the German Navy employed submarines primarily as commerce destroyers, while the British Navy employed them in conjunction with their surface fleet, as submerged sentinels near the German North Sea bases, and as patrols for certain areas frequented by German submarines. The British also constructed fleet submarines propelled by steam when on the surface which could sustain a speed of 20 knots; these formed an integral part of the Grand Fleet. The Germans were not successful in using their submarines in conjunction with their surface fleet. The notoriety gained by submarines operating against merchant ships has obscured their value as units of the fleet, a role in which, like aircraft and destroyers, they attain their maximum efficiency.

The Japanese have approximately 29 coastal submarines, of the "RO" class; these are comparable with 27 for the United States, 8 of the

"O" class and 19 of the "R" class. Of seagoing submarines Japan has 40, the United States 78. The Japanese, both torpedo and mine layer, are of the "I" and improved "I" class. These are larger and better than the American "S" class, but probably not as good as the *Nautilus, Pikes, Salmon* and *Sargos.* They are obviously intended to operate against American commerce along the Pacific coast, and are an excellent design for that purpose. With a radius of action of 16,000 miles, they can cross the Pacific and return to their own country without refueling. Thirteen improved "I's" were building when the American program of a two-ocean navy was announced. This number has probably been increased.

The "S" class of American submarines is smaller than the Japanese "I" class, but maneuverable and efficient. Although they have often cruised with the fleet, they are not entirely satisfactory fleet submarines for they cannot operate in all weathers.

All American submarines after the "V" class, rechristened the *Nautilus,* are capable of accompanying the fleet in all weathers, and average heavier than the Japanese "I" class. There are 9 of the *Nautilus* class, 4 *Pikes,*

6 *Perch,* 6 *Salmon,* 10 *Sargos* and 5 improved
Sargos, a total of 40 modern seagoing submarines. In addition, there were 7 improved
Sargos building when the two-ocean program
was decided upon. These should be completed
within a year. The first increment of the two-
ocean program included 73 submarines; the
total now building in the United States is 80.

Comparison of Japanese and American Submarines

JAPANESE	AMERICAN
Coastal	
29 "RO"	8 "O"
Surface displacement 650–1,000 tons	Surface displacement 480 tons
Surface speed 13–17 knots	Surface speed 11 knots
Submerged displacement 1,000–1,300 tons	Submerged displacement 624 tons
Submerged speed 9–10 knots	Submerged speed 8 knots
1 3-in. gun	1 3-in. gun
6 18-in. or 4–6 21-in. torpedo tubes	4 21-in. torpedo tubes
Cruising radius about 7,500 miles on surface	Cruising radius 3,500 miles on surface
	19 "R"
	Surface displacement 530 tons
	Surface speed 13 knots
	Submerged displacement 680 tons
	Submerged speed 10 knots
	1 3-in. gun
	4 21-in. torpedo tubes

Seagoing

34 "I"
  Surface displacement 1,100–
    2,000 tons
  Surface speed 14–21 knots
  Submerged displacement
    1,400–2,500 tons
  Submerged speed 9 knots
  1 5.5-in. gun or 1 4.7-in. gun
  6–8 21-in. torpedo tubes

  Cruising radius 16,000 miles

6 Improved "I's"

  Surface displacement 1,400–
    2,000 tons
  Submerged displacement
    2,000–2,600 tons

38 "S"
  Surface displacement 800–
    850 tons
  Surface speed 14–15 knots
  Submerged displacement
    1,100 tons
  Submerged speed 9 knots
  1 4-in. gun
  4 or 5 21-in. torpedo tubes
  12–14 torpedoes

40 ⎰ 9 *Nautilus* (formerly
   ⎱   "V's")
     4 *Pikes*
     6 *Perch*
     6 *Salmon*
     10 *Sargos*
     5 Improved *Sargos* built

  Surface displacement 1,100–
    2,700 tons
  Submerged displacement
    1,650–4,100 tons
  Surface speed 14–17 knots
  Submerged speed 8–11 knots
  3-in. to 6-in. guns
  6–10 21-in. torpedo tubes

69 Total   105 Total

Under Construction

13 Improved "I's." Number has   7 Improved *Sargos*, plus
   probably been increased   73 in two-ocean program

                                     80 Total

SUMMARY

Applying the American standard of obsolescence to both navies, their strengths in the five
categories are:

	JAPAN	UNITED STATES
Battleships	9	15
Aircraft carriers	6	6
Cruisers	32	37
Destroyers	126	160
Submarines	69	105

Omitting the *Arkansas* which carries 12-
inch guns, the battle line would be:

16-in. gun ships	2	67%	3	100%
14-in. (12 gun)	4	57%	7	100%
14-in. (8 gun)	3	75% (10 gun) 4	100%
Guns carried	24	60%	40	100%
Average in battle line		65%		100%

In aircraft carriers, including the *Hosho,*
which is obsolete according to American standards:

	7	117%	6	100%
Aircraft aboard carriers	280	60%	465	100%

In cruisers:

Heavy cruisers, 8-in. guns	12	67%	18	100%
Latest 6-in. gun cruisers	6	67%	9	100%
Oldest cruisers	14	140%	10	100%

It is difficult to compare these older cruisers but the Japanese are distinctly inferior to the American. It is approximately correct to place the over-all cruiser strength at:

	JAPAN	UNITED STATES
	70%	100%
Fast mine layers	3 3,000-ton cruisers	8 1,200-ton destroyers

In addition both navies have numerous slower mine layers and some fast mine sweepers; either cruisers or destroyers can be fitted as mine layers if the need for more should develop.

	JAPAN	UNITED STATES
Destroyers	126 79%	160 100%

Japanese destroyers are slightly smaller, slower and carry fewer torpedo tubes than do the American. With all destroyers present the Japanese could not fire in salvo as much as 70 torpedoes to 100 American. They are armed with 5.5-inch guns while Americans carry 5 inch. Under certain circumstances these heavier guns might be advantageous, but the experience of the last war convinced American destroyer officers that the 5-inch gun was as heavy as could be used advantageously on destroyers.

In addition Japan has about a dozen 500-ton torpedo boats built and 8 building that are useful only in coastal waters. Both navies are building some of the still smaller type of fast motorboats developed in Italy, and subsequently copied in Great Britain and Germany. This type is useful only in narrow waters and in conjunction with shore fortifications.

Both navies are well provided with destroyers for strictly fleet duties, and will commence hostilities with a surplus available for escort duties. Destroyers require frequent overhauls and suffer severe losses; after a few months' operations both navies would need more.

	JAPAN		UNITED STATES	
Total submarines	69	66%	105	100%
Coastal	29	107%	27	100%
Seagoing	40	51%	78	100%

Except off Japanese naval bases the American Fleet would have almost a 2 to 1 superiority in submarines, and off the entrance of the Inland Sea it could maintain a continuous submarine patrol. Japanese seagoing submarines can maintain themselves off Honolulu or along the Pacific coast. Japan and America have agreed to observe with submarines the rules of cruiser warfare, which prohibit the sinking of merchant ships without providing for the safety of the crews.

In each category except aircraft carriers the American Navy has a decided numerical superiority, and in numbers of planes carried the American Fleet has a 5 to 3 superiority. American ships are practically all in commission, reserve personnel has been called to active duty as needed and the navy is approaching a war footing. The Navy Department is prepared to man new ships as they are completed. The Japanese Navy is also practically in full commission and has been actively employed in the war with China. This war experience has given their aviation and landing force valuable training and the Japanese Navy would be well prepared to assist the Army in occupying Luzon. But employment in Chinese waters has interrupted the regular fleet training and the fleet will not be as well prepared for a naval engagement with the American Fleet as it was before the war. A similar diversion of the Atlantic Fleet to Mexican waters in 1914–15 seriously lowered its battle efficiency by interrupting the regular gunnery and tactical training.

The United States is building 17 battleships compared with an estimated 8 building in Japan. The U.S.S. *North Carolina* and the *Washington,* the first of the new program to be launched, were placed in commission in the spring of 1941, about six months ahead of the original schedule. Four other battleships were laid down in 1938–39, and are due to be completed in 1942 and 1943. The two-ocean-navy program includes 11 more, making a total of 17 battleships under construction in the United States.

The only basis for a reasonable estimate of Japan's building program is her known previous capacity to build, her probable capacity to increase these facilities, and the increased requirements of a modern battleship; for it is a fair assumption that Japan will increase her capital ships to the fullest extent compatible with the necessity of meeting her present war with China, preparing her army for possible eventualities in the western Pacific, and increasing other naval types.

In 1939 there were four yards in Japan which could construct capital ships: the two government yards at Yokosuka and Kure, the Mitubisi shipbuilding company at Nagasaki and the Kawasaki company at Kobe. It would be easy to construct shipbuilding slips at other yards, but it would be difficult and require time to provide the new slipways with the necessary equipment. Also it would be more difficult to provide the material needed for additional battleships. In 1920, when Japan's industry had been built up by the World War, when she was at peace and could concentrate her entire industry on her naval race with the United States, she launched only two battleships. Her heavy industries and her shipbuilding capacity have been greatly increased since then, but the demands upon them have been correspondingly increased by the exigencies of the war with China, the difficulty of obtaining material from abroad and the increasing complexity of shipbuilding. It is probable that Japan can construct four battleships or battle cruisers simultaneously and continuously without neglecting the construction of cruisers, destroyers and submarines.

Although she was free to do so, it is unlikely that Japan was able to lay down any capital ships in 1937; sixteen years had passed since battleships had been built; additional protection had to be provided against aircraft and submarines; general plans had to be agreed upon by the constructors, engineers and ordnance officers; detailed plans had to be drafted, and naval draftsmen were scarce in 1937. The Japanese Technical Division was fortunate if it was able to lay down two ships in 1938. According to Jane the Japanese program in 1937 provided for four battleships and one or two aircraft carriers to be completed by the end of 1942; and in 1939 provided 1,200,000,000 yen for new construction to be spent up to the end of 1945. In 1940 Jane credits Japan with two battleships, the *Nissin* and *Takamatu,* to be completed in 1941; and three others—one laid down in 1938, two in 1939.

In 1939 the Japanese Government probably revised its naval program to meet the two-ocean program of the United States, and prepared to increase its battleships in 1940. During 1940 it became increasingly difficult to obtain naval material abroad; and by the autumn of 1940 Japan probably was compelled to reconsider her capital ship program, for the events in Europe and the western Pacific developed more rapidly than anticipated and with them the danger of a collision with the United States before Japanese capital ships could be completed. If not, the passage of the Lend-Lease bill will compel the Japanese to decide between continuing construction on capital ships that might not be available to participate in a possible war with the United States in 1941–42 or concentrating the available labor and material on smaller craft. One thing is certain: Japan cannot carry out simultaneously a huge capital ship program and construction of cruisers, destroyers and submarines. Judging from previous Japanese plans and preparations to fight the United States, it is probable that Japan will subordinate her capital ship program to the smaller ships. Very likely she has deferred construction on all ships that cannot be completed by the end of 1942, and redoubled her efforts on the others. But Japan cannot entirely neglect her army and aviation; her industry will have to meet the demands for new planes and mechanized equipment for the army. Balancing the factors that enter into the Japanese problem, it is a fair estimate that Japan

Laid Down	Launched	Will Have Completed
Two battleships in 1938	in 1940	in 1942
Two battleships in 1939	in 1941	in 1943
Possibly two in 1940	in 1942	in 1944

By the autumn of 1940 the naval General Staff probably decided to defer work on the last two battleships and concentrate on the four further advanced. If this reasoning is correct, Japan has two battleships which may be completed in 1941 or early in 1942; two others which may be finished in the autumn of 1942 or early in 1943, and two others which have probably had little if any work done upon them.

The rumor that some of these are 45,000-ton battleships with 18-inch guns is improbable. But Jane reports the construction of 3 armored ships of 12,000 to 15,000 tons, armed with 6 12-inch guns, speed over 25 knots—an improved "pocket battleship." Such ships would have a nuisance value as surface raiders but could not join the battle line.

The United States is building 12 aircraft carriers: the *Hornet,* the nearest completion, was launched in December 1940; the Japanese are reported to be building 2 or 3. It can be assumed that they will increase their number of carriers on account of the American two-ocean program, but they will not try to equal the

United States for their naval position does not require as many.

The United States has contracted for 54 cruisers, 7 of which were laid down in 1940; the Japanese were reported to be building 6 when the two-ocean program was announced— they have probably increased that number. The United States is building 80 submarines and 204 destroyers, the Japanese were reported to be building 13 submarines and 11 destroyers but they have probably increased these numbers.

In addition to its initial numerical superiority in all but one category, the United States is building to the limit of its heavy industries and shipyards. Unquestionably Japan will do the same and the rapidity of naval replacements will depend upon the relative efficiency and capacity of American and Japanese industry. The naval campaign between the British and German Fleets in the North Sea during the World War began in the shipyards of the two nations about 1900 and culminated in Jutland. Whether the American Fleet could prosecute a campaign in the Far East with the utmost vigor would depend upon the efficiency of management and labor in American heavy industries as well as upon the officers and men of the United States Navy. If industry did its part, American naval superiority in ships would increase as the war proceeded.

The training program of the Navy Department already in operation will furnish crews for these new ships when finished. The Commander in Chief of the Pacific Fleet can depend upon a small but increasing number of replacements that would justify him in assuming and probably permit him to continue the offensive, enable him to carry the war to the Far East and to bring an ever-increasing pressure upon the Japanese people which might persuade them to abandon their efforts to establish Japanese hegemony in that area.

CHAPTER SIX

STRATEGY AND TACTICS

A T present the American Navy is organized in three fleets, the Atlantic, Pacific and Asiatic. The Pacific Fleet, formerly known as the United States Fleet, contains the bulk of the navy's fighting strength. The Panama Canal permits the Atlantic and Pacific Fleets to concentrate in either Caribbean or Hawaiian waters within three to four weeks. The Pacific and Asiatic Fleets can concentrate in Philippine waters in about three weeks; the three fleets can meet in Hawaiian waters in about four weeks. Smaller detachments of faster and larger ships could be transferred from one fleet to another in shorter time. Nevertheless it would be a strategic error to depend too much upon the Panama Canal and the mobility of ships.

Until the two-ocean navy is completed the navy should be concentrated in one fleet and kept in one ocean. At their present strengths,

the Pacific and Atlantic Fleets would need to
be brought together before undertaking a major campaign in either ocean; the period of
strained relations might not provide sufficient
time to effect their concentration; their concentration during a crisis might itself precipitate hostilities. These two considerations indicate the necessity of keeping the American
Navy at full strength in one fleet formation in
one ocean. The fleet may be in the Atlantic
when hostilities occur in the Pacific; even so,
it is a simpler and safer naval operation to
pass a concentrated fleet through the Canal or
through the Strait of Magellan than to effect a
junction of two fleets opposed by an enterpris-
ing enemy after hostilities begin. It would be
pure folly to commit this strategic error with
Japan a potential enemy, for she took full advantage of a similar mistake by Russia in
1904–5.

Dispersion of naval force is also a tactical error. On the day of battle the American Commander in Chief will need every combat ship;
he will grudge the absence of a single destroyer. His tactical objective is the decisive defeat and relentless pursuit of an enemy fleet.
Given a substantial numerical superiority

when the battle begins, he can achieve this re-sult with the least loss of American ships and sailors. After a war begins preparations for the decisive battle will govern the movements of the fleets; the peacetime organization and dis-position of American Fleets should be made to facilitate the wartime objective.

The present war in Europe added to the navy's responsibilities in the Atlantic and caused the department to increase the Atlantic Fleet at the expense of the Pacific until it in-cludes one division of battleships, a division of aircraft carriers, a division of heavy cruisers and numerous destroyers. It is strong enough to form an advance guard of the Pacific Fleet if that fleet is transferred to the Atlantic, or a rear guard if that fleet is transferred to the Far East. Any further increase in the Atlantic Fleet would seriously weaken the Pacific Fleet and would be difficult to justify.

The Pacific Fleet includes the Battle Force, the Scouting Force and the Base Force. The Battle Force is organized and trained for the specific purpose of attacking an enemy battle line; the Scouting Force to gain and maintain contact with an enemy fleet so that the Battle Force can bring it to action and destroy it; the

Base Force, sometimes called the "train," to service and supply the Battle and Scouting Forces.

The Asiatic Fleet consists of gunboats especially constructed for service on the rivers and inland waters of China to protect American lives and property in the interior of China, and a force of destroyers, submarines and aircraft to assist in the defense of Luzon. The ships assigned to Luzon can be considered an advance guard for the Pacific Fleet when it proceeds toward the Far East; initially they will be exposed to attack by superior Japanese forces, but they will greatly assist the army in Luzon if the Japanese attempt an invasion. Their detachment from the Pacific Fleet can be justified by the favorable tactical position they will enjoy in case Luzon is invaded, which will enable them to inflict much damage on Japanese ships supporting their army.

The usual tactical unit of the battle line is a division consisting of three battleships of approximately the same speed, armor and armament. A screen of destroyers always accompanies them to protect them from submarine attack; and at night a screen of destroyers and cruisers guards them against enemy destroyers.

They are protected from enemy planes by their antiaircraft batteries, their own and fleet fighting planes.

Aircraft carriers are assembled in divisions of two or three and similarly protected from submarines, destroyers and aircraft. Their own battleships protect them from enemy battleships or cruisers when they are with the fleet; when they are dispatched on independent duty a suitable escort of heavy cruisers or battleships must be provided. Planes from the carriers, battleships, cruisers and naval bases are organized in squadrons and wings.

The heavy cruisers are assembled in divisions and protected from submarines, destroyers and enemy aircraft like the battleships; they are fast enough to escape from enemy battleships and powerful enough to fight any other surface ship. The light cruisers are formed into divisions and with destroyer squadrons form the light forces of the Battle Force operating in unison with the battle line. They protect themselves from enemy light cruisers, destroyers, submarines and aircraft, being assisted by fleet fighting planes when attacked by enemy planes; they depend upon their heavy cruisers and battleships to protect them from enemy heavy cruisers; their speed enables them to escape enemy battleships. Certain light cruisers act as flagships of destroyer flotillas, and one serves as flagship of the Submarine Force of the Fleet.

Destroyers are formed into divisions of four. Two divisions form a squadron and with the destroyer flying the Squadron Commander's flag constitute a tactical unit of nine destroyers. Two squadrons form a flotilla which is furnished with a light cruiser for a flagship. All flotillas in the Battle Force are under the Commander of Destroyers Battle Force, those in the Scouting Force under the Commander of Destroyers Scouting Force. At night destroyers can take care of themselves; in daylight they depend upon their speed and a smoke screen to escape hostile battleships and cruisers by retiring upon their own cruisers and battleships; they rely upon their own antiaircraft batteries and fleet fighters to protect them against attacks from the air.

Submarines are formed into divisions, squadrons and a force, with a varying number in each formation. Some divisions are assigned to overseas bases—the Panama Canal and Pearl Harbor, Hawaii; others to the Asiatic,

Pacific and Atlantic Fleets. Submarines, by remaining submerged, can keep the sea in the immediate presence of greatly superior surface craft and aircraft; but they can undertake no action without exposing their periscopes. British submarines in the last war kept a periscope watch over Heligoland Bight and in the Kattegat, in spite of determined German offensives. Operating with the fleet, submarines can remain on the surface until the enemy craft are near; after an engagement they can sink disabled enemy ships that might otherwise escape.

The powers of all types of ships are enhanced and their limitations reduced when they are organized into a fleet. Each type makes its distinct contribution to the combined power and its own peculiar weakness has its compensation in the strength of other types. A combat ship of any type is a mass of concentrated power ready to respond to the will of its captain; a well-trained fleet is probably the greatest aggregation of power ever assembled that is instantaneously responsive to the will of one man—the Commander in Chief. With one signal Jellicoe could take the Grand Fleet in or out of port, day or night, in mist, fog or snow; another signal would place it in cruising formation, and another would deploy it for battle. Joffre articulated the mighty forces of the British and French Armies during battle by telephone, telegraph and dispatching staff officers in side cars to critical positions; Jellicoe controlled his fleet by visual and radio signals. The commander of a good fleet has at his immediate command ships designed to fight on and under the surface; he has fighting planes to protect his ships from bombers and torpedo planes, observation planes to scout and control the fire of his major batteries, bombing and torpedo planes to launch against enemy surface ships. The German Army rushing through the Low Countries in 1940 boasted of their latest tactical invention, a triple envelopment, from both flanks and the air; a skilful fleet commander can envelop both enemy flanks and attack simultaneously from under the sea and from the air.

Jellicoe integrated British submarines into the Grand Fleet; he used seaplane tenders and improvised short flight decks on top of his turrets to furnish him with aerial scouts. He created a magnificent weapon, but at Jutland his apprehensions prevented his full employment of it. Jellicoe's understandable anxieties need not torment the mind of the American commander operating in the western Pacific. He should relish a decisive day engagement. His fleet is initially stronger, the building program is larger, and American industry is more efficient in mass production than the Japanese. The Navy Department is providing personnel to man the new ships; he can depend upon a steady flow of fleet replacements. If the American Fleet suffered a tactical defeat, the continental United States could not be blockaded and the consequences of such a reverse would not be vital. An American victory over the Japanese Fleet, on the other hand, would be decisive; it would remove Japanese threats to the American position in the Far East and would isolate the Japanese Armies in eastern Asia as Nelson's victory at the Nile did Napoleon's army in Egypt. The bulk of the American Fleet could return to the Caribbean area, refit, repair damage, receive reënforcements, and in a very short time be ready for any major enterprise in the Atlantic.

The Commander in Chief of the Pacific Fleet is the senior naval officer afloat and in war takes command of the three American fleets. During peace he is given authority over

the other two Commanders in Chief to insure
uniformity of tactical training throughout the
navy. In wartime he is authorized to transfer
individual ships or fleet units from one fleet
or force to another. As all naval officers are
trained in the same system of tactics, these
transfers can be made without creating confusion, for every officer understands the tactical
concepts of the Commander in Chief of the
Pacific Fleet and can carry out the spirit of his
orders. After the fleets were concentrated in
wartime, it would frequently be necessary to
form temporary Task Forces for special under-
takings; these forces can be drawn from any
ships of the fleets, and when their particular
mission is performed they can be returned to
their original unit. The Commander in Chief
can regroup any of the naval forces, for he automatically takes command of all forces afloat
except those expressly excluded by the Chief
of Naval Operations.

The Japanese Combined Fleet is formed by
concentrating the First and Second Fleets into
one fleet under the Commander in Chief of
the First Fleet. The First Fleet with three divisions of battleships corresponds approximately

to the Battle Force of the American Pacific Fleet, the Second Fleet with its cruisers to the Scouting Force of the Pacific Fleet. The task of the First Fleet is to hold itself in readiness to attack the opposing fleet if its light forces can reduce the initial enemy superiority by minor attacks. The Second Fleet, which includes aircraft carriers, light and heavy cruisers, destroyers and submarines, must assist its submarines and aircraft in attacks on the enemy fleet and also endeavor to keep the Commander in Chief of the Combined Fleet informed of the condition, position, course and speed of the enemy fleet in order that he may decide whether or not he can risk a major engagement. The Japanese Fourth Fleet, based on the mandated islands, includes submarines, at least one seaplane tender with a minimum of 20 planes and equipped with catapults, and 2 squadrons of flying boats. The planes in the Fourth Fleet are probably below normal, for the Japanese Navy has furnished many of the planes employed against the Chinese Armies and cities during the current war; the supply, however, could be quickly replenished. Destroyers, torpedo boats and submarines would probably be added to the Fourth Fleet in a war with the

United States, and its task would be to gain the earliest information of the approach of the American Fleet for the Commander in Chief of the Combined Fleet. The commander of the Fourth Fleet would probably employ airplanes and submarines to discover the advance of the American Fleet, and would endeavor to keep informed of its rate of progress across the Pacific, in order to facilitate minor attacks by raiding forces.

The Marshall and Caroline Islands lie about two hundred miles south of the direct route to Guam from Honolulu. The American Fleet does not have to attack these islands or approach within one hundred miles of any Japanese island until it reaches the neighborhood of Guam. In these Japanese islands would be submarines, some Japanese flying boats and perhaps army bombers. Japanese submarines might be encountered by the American Fleet at any time it is at sea; but that is only a normal condition of sea warfare and no important unit of the American Fleet ever proceeds without its antisubmarine screen. In the last war the *U-29,* commanded by Lieutenant Commander Weddigen, one of the most skilful German submarine commanders, was rammed trying to attack a battleship of the Grand Fleet. No German submarine penetrated an American troop convoy when escorting destroyers were on their stations. The few successful submarine attacks were made when destroyers, through machinery breakdown or other causes, were off station. Japanese submarines are probably no better than the German; they would inflict losses, but not unbearable ones, and if they made determined attacks on the American Fleet their own losses would be heavy.

Japanese aviation might prove a more serious menace, but the air fields on Midway, Wake and Guam Islands, used by the Pan American Clippers, could supply continuous reënforcements of fighters and bombers for the American Fleet. These air bases are doubly valuable: they can provide reënforcements of planes for Manila and for any naval engagement that occurs in their vicinity. The United States Navy, under Rear Admiral William A. Moffett, took the lead in developing naval aviation and aircraft carriers. Japan has been energetic in her efforts to create naval aviation, but she is usually a phase behind. She cannot match in numbers the planes carried on American carriers and what is equally important, her personnel cannot send planes aloft or take them aboard as rapidly as American personnel. In the early part of a campaign Japan might compensate this disadvantage by using planes based upon the Mariana, Marshall and Caroline Islands. Special dispositions of the American Fleet would have to be made to meet that dangerous situation, and after the fleet was established in Manila the Japanese would, of their own accord, transfer those planes to the more active Philippine–South China area.

As has been said, the Japanese Combined Fleet will be commanded by the Commander in Chief of the First Fleet, just as all fleets of the United States would come under the Commander in Chief of the Pacific Fleet. The Japanese Chief of Staff in Tokio, however, would exercise more control over the movements of the fleet than would his American counterpart, the Chief of Naval Operations. The subdivisions of the Japanese and American Fleets are comparable in unit organization and in distribution of types. When concentrated, the two fleets will be similarly organized, the differences being chiefly in the number of units assembled. This similarity of fleet organizations has come about naturally, as a result of the

World War, in which both fleets developed their formations and tactical ideas. Then, a squadron of American battleships operated with the Grand Fleet in the North Sea while American destroyers operated generally with the British, French and Italian forces. Japan's active participation was not comparable to that of the United States: in the Grand Fleet she had only a number of observers and no ships; and only one division of Japanese destroyers served with the Allies, in the Mediterranean. In this way both American and Japanese naval officers kept themselves informed of the latest developments of naval warfare. Since the war, naval attachés of both countries have kept in touch with the most recent naval developments abroad and have applied the lessons learned to their own fleets. Thus it has come about that the two navies have almost kept step with each other.

The only naval weapon not thoroughly tested during the last war is the airplane. Some journalistic evidence of its powers and limitations during the Spanish Civil War and the present war can be offered but it must be accepted with reserve. A German pocket battleship was squarely hit by a heavy caliber bomb off the coast of Spain while at anchor with its watertight doors open. In spite of its exposed condition there was little structural damage done. During the present war the British Fleet steamed within easy bombing distance of a large concentration of heavy German bombers in Norway and Denmark, and the German Air Forces made a determined effort to sink the British capital ships. A battleship of the *Rodney* class was squarely hit on the forecastle by a bomb of the largest caliber. The two forward turrets were put out of action and a large hole made in the main deck, but the ship continued in the fight and did not leave the battle line, although she required docking and major repairs on reaching port. The evacuation of Dunkirk showed that with sufficient fighting planes and a willingness to accept losses, smaller vessels, cruisers and destroyers can maintain their stations for at least a week in the immediate presence of bombing planes. None of the actions between the British and Italian forces in the Mediterranean supports the theory that Italian submarines and aircraft can drive the British Fleet out of the Mediterranean. When German planes operate in large numbers in the Mediterranean the result may be different, but before this war few naval officers believed the British Fleet could maintain the offensive in sight of Italian air fields. The objectives of a naval war in the western Pacific would not compel an American Fleet to approach any Japanese air base as closely as the British Fleet has repeatedly approached Italian air bases.

While capital ships have not been sunk by air bombs, it is obviously perilous to operate them near heavy bombing squadrons. But land-based aircraft are not able to affect the movements of fleets at a distance from their air base. Naval formations, tactical dispositions and strategic plans have taken the air factor into account. New tactical formations will be evolved from the old by the ingenuity of the personnel using the new weapon.

If, contrary to the results in Europe, it should appear during a campaign in the western Pacific that heavy bombing planes were definitely superior to capital ships, the United States would still win the war. The political objective of protecting American and friendly interests in the western Pacific would be unchanged. The role of surface and air ships would be interchanged. American forces could gain and exercise control of the western Pacific

by making heavy bombers the principal offensive weapon against Japan rather than the battle line. American aviation excels Japanese
aviation in every branch;[1] it can operate from
the same bases as the fleet and from the Aleutian Islands. If aviation ever demonstrates its
superiority over surface craft, the United States

1. In design, contemporary American planes are faster,
more maneuverable and embody later improvements developed during the present war. American personnel have
more natural aptitude for flying and the numbers available
for training exceed the numbers available in Japan; American aviators are more thoroughly trained and American
naval aviators have led the world in naval and fleet aviation.

The American construction program, by providing British as well as American planes, has avoided accumulating a
surplus of 1939 and 1940 planes; the program has increased
the capacity of aviation plants in the United States and
made quantity production possible whenever a particularly
successful design is achieved or whenever the international
situation demands planes in quantity. While the factory capacity has been increased, experiments have been continued
and designers are obtaining increasingly better performance
by improving the bodies of the planes, increasing the
strength of materials used in construction, improving the
fuel used and the efficiency of the engines. The program of
"Aid to Great Britain" was primarily adopted to assist that
empire; it has worked to the advantage of the United States,
for the immediate need of American aviation in 1939 and
1940 was an ample supply of training planes for our young
aviators and an increased factory capacity. Both of these
needs have been met and they have been more easily met by
coöperation with the British program.

could defeat Japan with a superior air force as readily as with a superior navy.

Either the Japanese or the American Navy is prepared to resort to poison gas if the other is suspected of using it. During the Russo-Japanese War the Japanese were unjustly accused of using gas on account of the acrid fumes of the bursting charges in their armor-piercing shells. The Japanese and the American chemical industries can provide lethal gas if it is required.

From this comparison of the two fleets it is apparent that a naval campaign in the western Pacific would be a clash of two well-prepared navies, with ships of the same types, organized in similar formations, trained along similar lines, imbued with similar tactical ideas. The strategy would be affected by events in the Atlantic, which have already created the nucleus of an Atlantic Fleet and of a two-ocean navy.

The American Commander in Chief would begin the campaign with an initial superiority in all types of ships; if he could keep this superiority and concentrate his fleet on the day of battle he should be able to defeat the Japanese Fleet with little difficulty. If he could in-

flict equal or greater loss during the preliminary actions leading to the major engagement,
he would increase his relative superiority. His
best means of inflicting damage upon the
enemy is by waging a vigorous counteroffen-
sive against any ships that attempt to attack his
formation. He should not be content with
warding off blows; a vigorous counterattack is
the best defense against a Japanese war of attrition. His first task would be to transfer the
fleet to the Manila region, and during the latter part of the voyage he would have opportunities to attack Japanese detachments if they
attempted to raid the fleet. The time of passage
would depend upon the speed the slowest ship
can maintain in formation during the voyage.
With ships that could individually make 16
knots or better, $12\frac{1}{2}$ knots would be an average fleet speed for a voyage of 3,000 to 4,000
miles. This would mean a daily rate of 300 sea
miles. Under usual conditions of wind and
weather between Honolulu and Manila ships
can be refueled at sea, which adds to their total
cruising radius and raises the fleet's speed.

The fleet would be subject to air attacks
from the time it passed 170° east longitude until it arrived at its destination; these attacks

would continue during the remainder of the campaign in the Far East. But the fleet can defend itself with its own antiaircraft batteries and fighting planes. If it were attacked by Japanese heavy cruisers it could oppose them with a superior force of battleships, cruisers and bombing planes; if attacked by Japanese destroyers at night it could oppose superior light forces to them; if attacked by submarines in the day the ships would be defended by their own antisubmarine screen.

The movement of the American Fleet from Honolulu to the Luzon area would present some formidable tactical problems to the Commander in Chief. But they would be simpler than the difficulties that would confront the Japanese Commander in Chief, who must maintain the sea communications of the armies in Manchukuo, China and Indo-China, keep open the sea routes in the western Pacific to the Japanese islands, and as far as possible protect Japanese merchant shipping on the high seas. If the Japanese High Command decided to invade Luzon and Guam, the fleet must also support the landing operations of the army.

The Japanese technique in landing has probably improved with their experience in

China, but landings in Guam or Luzon would require naval support which would necessarily reduce the ships available to oppose the advance of the American Fleet. The Japanese could not employ the deliberate and prudent procedure used in the capture of Tsingtao in 1914; they must take Luzon and Guam promptly or the American Fleet might attack them while they were still landing their troops. If, to avoid losses among their newer ships, the Japanese used older ships to support these landings, their troops would be denied effective support by ships' batteries, for older ships lack modern fire-control equipment. The British experience at Gallipoli proved that the fire of ships without modern fire control, though enormous in volume, was ineffective when the invading infantry approached the entrenched defending infantry. At the critical moment when artillery support is most needed, the fire from old ships cannot be controlled accurately enough to continue shooting at the enemy without endangering friendly formations. If the ships' fire ceases the fire from machine guns and field artillery ashore that has been temporarily silenced reopens and becomes capable of inflicting heavy losses on the invading infantry. Should the Japanese support their army with their modernized battleships and new cruisers, these valuable ships would be exposed to minor attacks of American submarines, destroyers and aviation during the first part of the campaign.

The Japanese Commander in Chief would be compelled to employ a good many ships on scouting duty. At a minimum he must maintain scouting forces along the northern route from the Aleutian Islands, the middle route from Honolulu to Manila north of the Marshall and Caroline Islands, and the southern route from Honolulu to the southern Philippines south of those islands. These scouting forces would be widely deployed, and after the American Fleet was located all of them could not be assembled in time for a major engagement. The Japanese must take their scouting forces from their light cruisers, destroyers and armed merchantmen; they could not afford to deploy their battleships and heavy cruisers for this duty. Ships of the American Fleet are not limited to a defensive role. The probable position of the Japanese scouting forces could be calculated and they could be attacked by American cruisers and plane carriers. In addition, American naval aviation can attack the sea and air bases of the Japanese mandated islands or the Japanese islands themselves. Army bombers based on the Aleutian Islands would be a continuous threat to the industrial plants concentrated around the Inland Sea, and American seagoing submarines would be as ubiquitous as the Japanese and would have equally good information of the disposition of Japanese forces.

If an army or naval commander submitted a plan of attack that deliberately separated his forces and ordered them into action in small groups on each successive morning or after each twilight, the tactical instructor at an elementary military school would condemn the plan as unsound. The proposed harassing attacks by successive detachments of the Japanese Fleet on the American Fleet en route to the Far East are minor attacks by inferior forces on a well-organized superior force and nothing more. If Japanese cruisers, destroyers, submarines and aircraft were deployed in groups in the mandated islands and along the route between Honolulu and Manila, the American Navy could not ask for a more favorable disposition of the enemy forces. Ashore, generals maneuver for days and accept heavy initial losses to separate an enemy army into small parts in order to destroy them in detail; if Japan should obligingly scatter her light forces, submarine and aircraft, across the middle Pacific, the American Commander in Chief should be grateful to his opponent. The quickest way to win the war would be to destroy the Japanese Fleet, and if it were sent into action piecemeal it could be destroyed more easily.

The Japanese Commander in Chief is probably too intelligent to disperse his forces widely. If he wished to reduce the initial American superiority by attacks of his light forces, he must deploy them ahead of his main body of capital ships, and then hold his main body in a position close at hand ready to follow up a successful attack of his light forces. But whenever the main body comes near enough to the American Fleet to follow up a blow of its light forces, it exposes itself to attacks by American submarines, airplanes, destroyers and finally to an attack by the main body of the American Fleet.

If the Japanese Fleet followed closely behind its light forces and were encouraged by their minor successes, it might accept a major engagement in the early part of the campaign. A Japanese invasion of Guam and Luzon would increase the chances of a fleet engagement by tying the Japanese Fleet to its army, for the naval commander would not relish the idea of retiring to the security of the Inland Sea and abandoning the army's line of communication to attacks of the American Fleet. The American commander wants to fight a decisive engagement at the earliest moment possible and would be glad to learn during the voyage that the Japanese were landing in Luzon.

But the Japanese commander may well wish to delay a major engagement until he has had an opportunity to reduce the initial American superiority by minor attacks of his destroyers, submarines and aircraft. Yet to take full advantage of any successes of his light forces he must bring his fleet nearer to the scene of probable action than the Inland Sea, and his light forces must endeavor to compensate for the relative inactivity of the battle line by increased exertions. These two Japanese necessities would develop numerous tactical situations which would offer opportunities for

American counterattacks with the light forces using guns, torpedoes, mines and bombs. During these encounters the American Fleet, being the stronger, should seek battle on all occasions and in all waters except along the coast of Japan and its overseas bases. It would prefer a major engagement in the early part of the campaign and a chance to end the war at a blow; if this were not possible, every minor engagement with Japanese naval forces should be welcomed. A commander of any unit or task force of the American Navy will not go wrong if he engages decisively any enemy detachment of the same or slightly greater strength; he would need only to inflict seven tenths of the loss he received to preserve the general ratio of Japanese-American Fleet strength. If he inflicted as much damage as he received the American Fleet would gain in the ratio of 10 to 7. Every loss inflicted on a Japanese detachment would make it increasingly difficult for the inferior Japanese Fleet to carry on the war.

If the Japanese Fleet were unwilling to accept a major engagement, the American Fleet would have to fight only a series of minor engagements to reach Manila. It would be in radio communication with the Commander in Chief of the Asiatic Fleet and the Commanding General of the Philippine Department, and would know the conditions at Guam and Manila from day to day; air and submarine re-enforcements could meet the fleet as it approached Guam. From the region of Guam it would be possible to reach Manila passing north of Luzon or via San Bernardino Strait; or, if necessary, the fleet could proceed to a temporary roadstead in the southern Philippines. It would have a choice of three terminal routes and thus retain freedom of maneuver as long as its fuel lasted. The Japanese Fleet could always interpose between it and Manila, if they were willing to fight a decisive action in the Manila area. They probably would not be, for they would be 1,500 miles from any dry dock large enough to take a damaged capital ship. The American Fleet would certainly be allowed to use the dry docks at Singapore and there is a floating dock at Olongapo large enough for all except capital ships. Thus it would have an advantage over the Japanese in so far as damaged cruisers and smaller ships were concerned, if the fight took place near Manila.

The American Fleet would cross the Pacific at about the speed of translation of a cyclone—between 10 and 15 knots. It would resemble the cyclone in a more important phase, leveling everything in its path except a stronger fleet—and a stronger fleet does not at present exist. Moreover, the American Fleet belongs to a continental nation that can risk it in battle without jeopardizing the national security. The United States is the only continental nation since Imperial Rome and Spain under Charles V to have a preponderant navy. The Commander in Chief of the Japanese Navy would fight knowing that the defeat of his fleet would seal the doom of his country. That thought haunted Jellicoe; it will not stimulate the Japanese Commander in Chief.

Established in Manila, the American Fleet can maintain a long-range blockade of Japan by intercepting all vessels headed for Japan or North China as they come through the straits entering the South China Sea. Diplomatic difficulties will not interfere with the enforcement of this blockade; all nations that need to be considered are either belligerent or have declared their intentions of favoring one side or the other. All ships east of Suez steering for

Japan or steaming from the South Seas or the west coast of America can be stopped. The only problem confronting the Commander in Chief would be the tactical one of resisting the war of attrition and keeping the fleet ready to fight the Japanese Fleet if it came out of harbor.

Simultaneously the fortifications and garrisons in Luzon and Guam should be strengthened and provisioned until they could resist a Japanese attack for at least a year. At last Congress has withdrawn its opposition to the fortification of Guam and in all probability the defenses of that strategic island will be increased. Then if it became necessary for the American Fleet to return to the Atlantic before defeating the Japanese, the protection of Luzon and Guam could be safely entrusted to the army during its absence. The War Department has officially announced that it has available 700,-000 troops and during 1941 this force will be increased to 1,500,000. If sufficient garrisons are used in the Pacific they will keep possible enemies thousands of miles from the continental United States.

The Japanese and American Fleets possess similar weapons, and can undertake similar operations. Japanese submarines can attack American surface ships, and American submarines can attack Japanese surface ships. Japanese aviation can attack American ships, American aviation can attack Japanese ships. Submarine enthusiasts in all navies are convinced that the submarine is invincible. Destroyer officers are equally certain they can break through any enemy screen and send any battleship to the bottom. Cruiser captains are confident they can penetrate an enemy screen and obtain information for the Commander in Chief. Battleship crews are convinced that they can withstand submarine, destroyer, or air attacks and sink enemy battleships. A wise Commander in Chief will agree with them all and encourage the faith that each commander has in his own ship. The difference in the skill of the opposing personnel can make all these contradictory statements come true. A skilful submarine commander can penetrate a destroyer screen; an alert destroyer captain can sink the submarine; a resourceful commander of a destroyer squadron can successfully attack battleships; in the same fleet one battleship can make twice as many hits at target practice as a sister ship. As weapons become more precise and deadly a higher degree of competence is required to use them, but with that competence must go the faith that good soldiers and sailors always have in their regiments and their ships; without that faith, skill is not enough.

Neither the Japanese nor the American Navies were pitted against first-class personnel in their wars with Russia and Spain. They acquitted themselves well during the World War, but neither was severely tried. The Japanese displayed intelligence and proper circumspection in their attacks on Tsingtao. American battleships and destroyers did excellent service in the European war zone, but were not subjected to the ordeal of a three-dimensional battle. It has been twenty-three years since the American Navy was at war, and during that interval the Japanese Fleet has been employed only in supporting an army on hostile shores and using its aviation against the Chinese Army. Their recent war experience affords little direct evidence of the comparative efficiency of the personnel of either fleet. It is known that both navies have energetically and systematically prepared themselves for battle. The Japanese and American people have entire confidence in the personnel of their fleets, but the available evidence indicates that the American people have better reasons for the faith that their navy will emerge victorious.

As the blockade progressed the Japanese Commander in Chief might be compelled by public opinion to offer battle; attacks by American bombing planes may persuade him to leave the Inland Sea; or during some sweep of the American Fleet toward Japan a chance encounter of light forces may result in a major action. Whatever brings it about, a major naval engagement would probably begin with air fights between bombing and torpedo planes seeking to attack capital ships, observation planes trying to gain information and fighting planes attempting to drive them off. Each Commander in Chief would with the scanty information available maneuver to gain a superior tactical position; the American commander would seek to interpose between the Japanese and their nearest base to insure a decisive fight; the Japanese commander would endeavor to keep his line of retreat open. But the American commander should not waste much time in maneuvers. The best way to insure a decisive battle is to disable some of the

Japanese capital ships, and thus compel the commander to stay and fight or abandon his crippled ships.

The air engagements may be accompanied, and they would certainly be followed by clashes between opposing light forces in the van of each fleet, seeking to gain information and a favorable position to attack the head of the enemy line. Closely behind the light forces will come the capital ships, which will deploy from their cruising formations into the battle formations and fire their ranging salvos. The battle line that begins to hit before being hit will naturally gain a great advantage. At extreme ranges the heavy armor will protect the vital parts of the ships, but as the range is closed even the heaviest armor will be penetrated. And the hits will have a cumulative effect. When the battle lines are heavily engaged, either commander may launch an attack by the light forces which have been maneuvering to gain a favorable tactical position. As the light forces of both sides are animated by the same desire, their maneuvering will result in a series of engagements almost midway between the opposing battle lines, comparable in many respects to the day engagements between Beatty's and Hipper's light forces in the opening phase of the battle of Jutland.

If either battle line suffers heavily from the other's gunfire, its commander may order all the light forces to attack the head of the enemy battle line in full force, regardless of losses, in order to create a diversion and open the range. Scheer found himself under such a necessity when the British battleships began to pound his weaker battle line at Jutland. Under cover of the attack of his light forces Scheer extricated his battleships from the deadly embrace of the Grand Fleet. The speed of the battle line averages less than 20 knots, of the light forces over 30 knots; the scene of the battle will change rapidly and if it lasts several hours it will cover at least 50 miles and probably more.

Fast mine layers with the light forces will endeavor to lay their explosive cargoes in the path of advancing enemy forces. They must lay them circumspectly or they will block the advance of their own forces; and as their cargoes are small and the area of the battle large, they will not be very effective. Submarines will have better opportunities; they can range with

little danger in their search for disabled enemy
ships to sink. The importance of giving the
finishing stroke is frequently forgotten—a
badly damaged capital ship if it reaches port
can be repaired within three or four months,
but it will require as many years to construct a
new capital ship. If the commander has some
bomber or torpedo planes on hand they can assist the submarines in dealing the death blow
to disabled ships too helpless to protect themselves.

Over the confused and shifting battle scene
will hang heavy columns of smoke from fast-
moving ships and from screens deliberately
laid by destroyers or aircraft for tactical purposes. Disabled ships will be dropping out of
formation, divisions will be broken, but the
remaining ships will re-form. Ships' crews have
repeatedly rehearsed their parts in this great
drama; officers have been familiarized with all
its possibilities until they are mentally prepared for any form the battle may take. On this
great occasion many of them will unconsciously
have that sensation of having been through it
all before which inspired Rear Admiral Mad-
den, Jellicoe's Chief of Staff at Jutland, to say
to the Commander in Chief, as the Grand Fleet

steamed at full speed to support Beatty's battle cruisers, "This is all going according to expectation." And if the American Commander in Chief recalls the assertion of Joffre that "battles can and should be controlled," he will find the means to give orders to the units of the fleet, give form to the battle, and dominate the whole scene and the mind of his adversary. That is the final necessity, for the ships are but the instrument. The American commander must convince the Japanese commander that he has met his master. Then victory will be assured.

During the last phase of a sea battle the defeated fleet can be cut to pieces. The Commander in Chief has trained and husbanded his forces for that purpose. It was to destroy the enemy fleet that he zealously guarded his initial numerical superiority and maneuvered to gain a superior tactical position; for this purpose he laboriously trained his gun and torpedo crews and exercised his fleet at tactics, and he should not fail to reap the full fruits of his victory. The good ordinary admiral will be content with a partial success, he will be oppressed by his own losses and satisfied to gather together his own scattered forces; he will have done well enough for one day. Not so a Nelson, a Perry, a Farragut, a Sampson or a Dewey; only the destruction of the entire enemy fleet will satisfy such a commander, who will pitilessly pursue the fleeing enemy, reforming his forces and urging his own tired crews to the supreme effort in order to crush the enemy beyond hope of rehabilitation.

CHAPTER SEVEN

CONCLUSION

IN spite of the numerous land, sea and air forces now under arms in Europe, Asia, Africa and Australasia, its geographical position and potential military strength will permit the United States to choose its foreign policy provided it proceeds with its armament program. Neither Germany nor Japan wishes to fight the United States under existing circumstances but either of them might fight if the United States interfered seriously with their plans for a new order. Today Americans can stand aside and leave the remainder of the world to its own devices, they can limit their activities to the Western Hemisphere, or they can take a decisive part in the affairs of the world. The present generation of Americans has a free choice.

Americans can abandon their interests abroad, restrict their energies to their own country and gradually become a self-sufficient hermit nation; their virility, their genius for organization, their industry and their well-recognized military capacity would deter any nation from objecting to their voluntary retirement from the world scene. This course would require the complete abandonment of American interests overseas and all efforts to protect Americans who ventured abroad. The people of the United States would not find complete isolation congenial; eventually they would return to the world of their own accord as the Japanese did, or possibly be dragged back as some Asiatic countries were.

Americans can pursue a middle course; they can abandon their interests in Europe, Asia, Africa and Australasia, restrict their activities to the Western Hemisphere, and provide for its protection with their own army and navy. This policy would require close coöperation with all Central and South American countries, including, at a minimum, provision for adequate naval and air bases at strategic positions, and permission to land an American expeditionary force in their territories if it was required to repel an attack from Europe or Asia on any part of the Americas. The United States would have to support a two-ocean navy with corresponding increases in naval aviation; an army expeditionary force, with motorized equipment and heavily reënforced aviation units; and maintain army missions and nucleus garrisons in naval and air bases in Latin America. By accepting responsibility for the defense of the Western Hemisphere the United States would increase the cost of its armed forces; in return it would in effect reserve Central and South America for its future development. By restricting its efforts to the Americas it would reduce the chance of immediate involvement in war with Germany or Japan.

Such a policy would be defensive and could be supported by defensive strategy, but its cost would be enormous. If Great Britain is defeated, to defend the eastern shores of the Western Hemisphere the American Fleet in the Atlantic would have to equal the fleet Germany can build with the heavy industries and the shipbuilding resources of western Europe operating under her socialized economy and totalitarian government. To defend the western shores of the Western Hemisphere from a Japanese attack, using the Aleutian, Hawaiian and Galapagos Islands as outposts, would require an American Fleet in the Pacific as large

as Japan could maintain with her own resources, supplemented by raw materials obtained in Asia and Malaya, supplying her
heavy industries and her shipbuilding plants,
operated by her own and other Asiatic cheap
labor. American Army and Navy aviation
might have to equal the air forces of Japan and
Germany, for they could choose the time of attack and synchronize their operations. The
completion of this naval and air program
would take six years, and before it was accomplished many of the airplanes and some of the
small naval craft would be obsolete; a replacement program would begin before construction was finished. In fifteen years cruisers and
destroyers, in twenty years battleships would
have to be replaced. The total cost of material
would be staggering, but it would probably be
less than the cost of the personnel at air fields,
army and navy shore establishments and in the
army and navy ranks. The middle way will
avoid complete isolation and reduce temporarily the danger of being involved in war, but
its peacetime cost would change the domestic
economy and present form of American life.

Americans can choose the bold way; they
can announce their determination to support

China and Great Britain to the limit of their resources, even if it involves war with Japan and Germany. Obviously the risk of war would be increased but war itself will be no more disastrous to the American way of life than a prolonged armament race with Germany and Japan, followed by an armed truce of indefinite duration. The bold way offers a last opportunity to avoid making the difficult choice between complete isolation, consuming the nation's manhood and wealth in endless preparation for war, and war. While accelerating the armament program, the American Government may be able to convince the Japanese Government that they have no desire to deny Japan the raw materials necessary to her economic life as an industrialized nation, but are determined to prevent the indefinite political expansion of Japan in the western Pacific. A compromise solution is feasible. There are sufficient raw resources available to Japan in the Far East without dispossessing the present landowners. There is an eleventh-hour chance to convince the Japanese leaders they have unnecessarily identified a real need for access to raw materials and markets with a fictitious need for more territory. Japanese commercial expansion during the past quarter of a century proves she can more than hold her own with her foreign competitors.

Sober second thoughts on the part of Japanese and American leaders and peoples have helped them through dangerous crises in the past. If the Japanese leaders—military, naval, diplomatic, financial, industrial and commercial—pause to consider their situation, they should realize that it would be easier for them to meet British and American competition than German; it would be simpler to adjust their economic system with that of Great Britain and the United States than it would be to compete with the compulsions of the German barter arrangements. There will be more lasting and valuable opportunities for Japanese commerce in world markets in which Great Britain and the United States are powerful factors than in a world economic system dominated by Berlin. American leaders can make it plain to Japan that American interests would not be prejudiced by a flourishing Japan and that they have no incentive to deny Japan her full share in the affairs of the Far East; they do not propose, however, to have their interests in the Far East blotted out in a Japanese-dominated Greater Asia.

If Japanese leaders reject these overtures it will indicate that under the guise of securing raw materials they have determined to establish a Japanese Empire limited only by their armed strength. They will continue to follow the initiative of Berlin and it will be correspondingly difficult to prevent war between the two countries unless the United States precipitately abandons all its interests in the western Pacific. Otherwise Japan's continued collaboration with Germany will force closer cooperation between Great Britain and the United States, which in turn might conceivably involve the United States in a war in the Atlantic during which Japan would have a comparatively free hand in the Far East. With the main strength of the British and American Fleets in the Atlantic, there would still remain enough British, American and Dutch submarines and aircraft in the Pacific to inflict considerable damage on the Japanese Fleet, the Chinese Army would increase its resistance and Japan would be unable to effect the speedy capture of American, British and Dutch strongholds. Japanese naval officers know that any overseas conquests are temporary as long as the enemy fleets remain undefeated; they can expect but little assistance from Germany in a naval war in the Pacific with the Anglo-American Navies supported by their overseas bases in the Pacific and their superior resources. They also realize better than their army officers that once involved in war the American people will fight to a finish. It is no reflection on Japanese military genius, courage or patriotism to say that a sober estimate of the situation should convince leaders in Japan that they could not reasonably hope to defeat the United States, whose population, resources and military position are superior to their own. There are no economic reasons that could justify the Japanese Government in accepting the hazards of war with the United States, and there is no need for an army or navy which has already shown its valor in a score of battles to embark upon a desperate war to prove its prowess.

If the United States continues its preparations for war while giving Japan every honorable opportunity to avoid hostilities, it will reduce the chances of war to a minimum consistent with its own national safety; and if nevertheless war ensued, Americans could enter upon it with the conviction that it was not of their making and with no apprehensions of the outcome. Whatever temporary successes Japan might have in the western Pacific, her final defeat would be inevitable. The continental position of the United States with its outlying insular bulwarks is invulnerable to any Japanese attack, sooner or later the American Navy would return in full force to the Pacific, and the thickly populated, highly industrialized island empire would be doomed. The new weapons, submarines and aviation would only hasten her end; the submarines would tighten the blockade and aircraft would compel her weaker fleet to come out and meet its fate at sea or be bombed into helplessness in the Inland Sea.

APPENDIX

THE PRESIDENT
Commander in Chief of the Army and Navy

The Secretary of War — The Joint Board — Secretary of the Navy

Chief of Staff of the — The Joint Planning — The Chief of Naval
Army   Committee   Operations

The War Council   The Secretary's Council

The President commands the army through the Secretary of War, the navy through the Secretary of the Navy. He provides for joint army-navy action by means of the Joint Army and Navy Board in Washington, whose Joint Planning Committee is in continuous operation in peace and war preparing general directives which govern both the army and navy. Under the Joint Board in Washington are functional joint boards, such as the Joint Aeronautical and Ordnance Boards. Coöperation outside of Washington is provided by local joint boards at corps area and naval district headquarters, and overseas, by joint boards at department and naval district headquarters. Coöperation between the Commanding General and the Commander in Chief in time of war would be provided in a general directive of the President, details of which would have been prepared by the Joint Board in Washington; different phases of the campaign would be coördinated in accord with the general directive by means of liaison officers exchanged between the commanding officers.

In the Panama Canal Zone, in Hawaii, and in the Philippines the army and navy commands have functioned together regularly for years; there are frequent disagreements but there is machinery to settle them and continued association is the best means of securing harmony of action, for many apparent differences disappear when discussed in a friendly manner. But sincere and irreconcilable professional differences will occur; these have to be settled by the Joint Board in Washington, or by the President in case the board cannot agree.

Ashore the army has command of all army and navy forces operating together; at sea the navy has command. During landing operations the navy is responsible for the passage overseas and getting the troops ashore. Once the troops are ashore and able to take care of themselves, the army commander takes over, but the navy is still responsible for protecting the overseas communications. In a joint expedition the problem of command may arise but the machinery to settle it is provided and the President as Commander in Chief has absolute authority.

INDEX

A R M E D

OF THE